EGO GOES: DIVINITY GROWS

DEATH OF THE EGO IS BIRTH OF THE DIVINE LIFE

J. P. VASWANI

Published by:
GITA PUBLISHING HOUSE
Sadhu Vaswani Mission,
10, Sadhu Vaswani Path,
Pune - 411 001, (India).
gph@sadhuvaswani.org

EGO GOES: DIVINITY GROWS
©2015, J. P. Vaswani
ISBN : 978-93-80743-91-2

First Edition

DADA VASWANI'S BOOKS
Visit us online to purchase books on self-improvement, spiritual
advancement, meditation and philosophy.
Plus audio cassettes, CDs, DVDs, monthly journals and books in Hindi.
www.dadavaswanisbooks.org

Printed by:
Jayant printery
352/54, Girgaum Rd, Murlidhar Temple Compound
Near Thakhurdwar P.O., Mumbai - 400 002
Tel: 022-43667171
jayantprintery@gmail.com

EGO GOES: DIVINITY GROWS

J. P. VASWANI

Gita Publishing House,
Pune, (India).
www.dadavaswanisbooks.org

Other Books and Booklets by J.P. Vaswani

In English:

7 Commandments of the Bhagavad Gita
10 Commandments of a Successful Marriage
108 Pearls of Practical Wisdom
108 Simple Prayers of a Simple Man
108 Thoughts on Success
114 Thoughts on Love
A Little Book of Life
A Little Book of Wisdom
A Simple and Easy Way to God
A Treasure of Quotes - Vol. I
A Treasure of Quotes - Vol. II
Around the Camp Fire
Be An Achiever
Be in the Driver's Seat
Begin the Day with God
Bhagavad Gita in a Nutshell
Burn Anger Before Anger Burns You
Comrades of God - Lives of Saints from East & West
Daily Appointment with God
Daily Inspiration (A Thought for Every Day of the Year)
Daily Inspiration
Destination Happiness
Dewdrops of Love
Does God Have Favourites?
Empower Yourself
Face It With Love
Finding Peace of Mind
Formula for Prosperity
Friends Forever
Gateways to Heaven
God in Quest of Man
Good Parenting
Happily Ever After
How to Overcome Depression
I am a Sindhi
I Luv U, God!
Immortal Stories
India Awake
Joy Peace Pills
Kill Fear Before Fear Kills You
Ladder of Abhyasa
Lessons Life Has Taught Me
Life after Death
Life and Teachings of Sadhu Vaswani
Life and Teachings of the Sikh Gurus: Ten Companions of God
Living in the Now
Management Moment by Moment
Mantra for the Modern Man
Mantras for Peace of Mind
Many Paths: One Goal

Many Scriptures: One Wisdom
Moment of Calm - Desk Calendar
Nearer, My God, to Thee!
New Education Can Make the World New
Peace or Perish: There Is No Other Choice
Practise the Presence of God
Positive Power of Thanksgiving
Questions Answered
Saints for You and Me
Saints With a Difference
Say No to Negatives
Secrets of Health and Happiness
Seven Steps on the Path
Shake Hands With Life
Short Sketches of Saints Known & Unknown
Sketches of Saints Known & Unknown
Spirituality in Daily Life
Stay Connected
Stop Complaining: Start Thanking!
Swallow Irritation Before Irritation Swallows You
Teachers are Sculptors
The Endless Quest
The Goal of Life and How to Attain It
The Highway to Happiness
The Little Book of Freedom from Stress
The Little Book of Prayer
The Little Book of Service
The Little Book of Success
The Little Book of Yoga
The Magic of Forgiveness
The New Age Diet: Vegetarianism for You and Me
The Perfect Relationship: Guru and Disciple
The Simple Way
The Terror Within
The Way of Abhyasa (How to Meditate)
Thus Have I Been Taught
Tips for Teenagers
What You Would Like to Know About Karma
What You Would Like to Know About Hinduism
What to Do When Difficulties Strike: 8 easy Practical Suggestions
Why Do Good People Suffer?
Why Be Sad?
WOMEN: Where Would the World be Without You?
You Are Not Alone: God Is With You!
You Can Change Your Life: Live— Don't Just Exist!

Story Books:

100 Stories You Will Never Forget
101 Stories For You And Me

25 Stories For Children and also for Teens
It's All A Matter of Attitude
Snacks For the Soul
More Snacks For the Soul
Break the Habit
The Heart of a Mother
The King of Kings
The Lord Provides
The One Thing Needful
The Patience of Purna
The Power of Good Deeds
The Power of Thought
Trust Me All in All or Not at All
Whom Do You Love the Most?
The Miracle of Forgiving
You Can Make A Difference

In Hindi:

Aalwar Santon Ki Mahan Gaathaayen
Aapkay Karm, Aapkaa Bhaagy Banaatay
Atmik Jalpaan
Atmik Poshan
Bhakton Ki Uljhanon Kaa Saral Upaai
Bhale Logon Ke Saath Bura Kyon?
Chaahat Hai Mujhe Ik Teri Teri
Dainik Prerna
Dar Se Mukti Paayen
Ishwar Tujhe Pranam
Krodh Ko Jalayen Swayam Ko Nahin
Laghu Kathayein
Mrityu Hai Dwar... Phir Kya?
Prarthana ki Shakti
Sadhu Vaswani: Unkaa Jeevan Aur Shiks
Safal Vivah Ke Dus Rahasya
Santon Ki Leela
Sarvottam Sambandh
Shama Karo Sukhi Raho
Srimad Bhagavad Gita: Gagar Mei Sagar

Other Publications:

Books on J. P. Vaswani:

A Pilgrim of Love
Dada J.P. Vaswani's Historic Visit to Sin
Dost Thou Keep Memory
Guru of None, Disciple of All
How To Embrace Pain
Interviews and Innerviews
Jiski Jholi Mein Hain Pyaar
Life and Teachings of Dada J.P. Vaswani
Living Legend
Moments with a Master
Pyar Ka Masiha

Contents

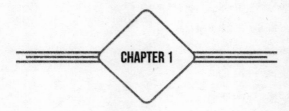

CHAPTER 1

WHO IS "I"?

Nobody can teach me who I am. You can describe parts of me, but who I am - and what I need - is something I have to find out myself.

- Chinua Achebe

The Bird in the Cage

There was a bird who lived in a cage. For as long back as he could remember, he had always lived in a cage. It was the only kind of life he knew. He thought this was how all birds lived.

The cage was quite roomy and comfortable. He could move around freely. He hopped from one corner to the other, undertaking regular inspection tours of his cage. But he could not flutter his wings about, or fly. The floor of the cage was cleaned regularly and fresh straw, grass and twigs were left for him. Berries, fruits and other juicy tidbits were regularly supplied to him along with fresh water. He was quite content in his cage.

Just to keep himself busy, he started building himself a nest with the straw and twigs left in the cage. He was very proud of the nest. As days passed, he found other distractions to occupy him. The only thing was that he could not try out his wings. But that was alright, since his life was otherwise quite comfortable.

One day, during his regular inspection of the cage, he was taken aback to find a hinge and a door attached to it! It was the same cage he had always lived in; it had not changed at all; but he had been quite, quite, unaware that the cage had a door! Puzzled and intrigued, the bird fiddled with the door. The latch came undone, and the door opened. The bird stared in amazement at the opening. But he made no attempt to leave the cage.

He could have done this anytime earlier; but it hadn't occurred to him to do so. Now, he stared into freedom. There had never been any constraints on him; it was just that he was not aware of his situation. The bird perched at the threshold and just stared ahead of him. Which was better and safer? The cage or freedom?

You are Not the Body, the Mind and the Senses.

Alas, the world judges people by outward appearances. Go anywhere – and you are judged by the clothes you wear, the car you drive, even your hairstyle. Your exterior is what counts!

If you wish to understand your true self, you must stop identifying yourself with the body, the mind and the senses. You must move away from the "shoes" you wear. This is indeed the significance of the custom practised by Hindus – removing one's shoes before one enters a temple or a holy place. This is symbolic of the idea that we move away from body-consciousness to walk upon the sanctified ground, which will help us move towards God-realisation.

We cannot cast off the body, literally. But we can change our perspective by dwelling on the idea that we are not the bodies we wear – we are the immortal spirits within. This makes a tremendous change in our outlook!

The Bible tells us of the young man who approached Jesus and asked to be his follower. When Jesus spoke to him of the Ten Commandments, he assured the Master that he had been observing them for several years. Then Jesus said to him, "If you wish to enter the kingdom of Heaven, then sell everything you have, and come and follow me."

The young man was not prepared to do this. He backed away, not without regret.

Selling everything one has is not to be interpreted literally. It too means moving away from the ego, from identification with the body.

So ask yourself again and again: who am I?

According to Vedanta philosophy, as human beings, all of us wear the garment of the physical body, our outer form of matter. This is the *annamayakosha*. Within this outer sheath is the *prana* or vital breath, which constitutes the *pranamayakosha;* our mind, or the instrument of cognition, along with the senses or the *indriyas,* constitutes the *manonmayakosha;* the ego and the intellect, together, constitute our *vignanamayakosha;* the consciousness of pure bliss is the innermost sheath, the *anandamayakosha*: folded in the centre of the five sheaths resides the true self – that *which is*. Caught up as we are in the mire of worldly existence, most of us rarely experience this bliss or indeed become aware of the true self within us.

The sad truth is we live most of the time in the consciousness of the body alone!

We are obsessed with appearances.

I hope I look good; this dress suits me; I need to 'do' my hair; I have really become dark with sun tan; I've got to lose weight; I hope my grey hair is not showing; I think I should go in for cosmetic surgery/ dental implants/ liposuction...

We are slaves to the palate.

I shall have pizza today; I really don't like Indian food; vegetarian food is so boring; I prefer Italian ice cream; I don't like spinach/ cabbage/ broccoli/ sweet potatoes/ pumpkin...

We expect to be in perfect health and fitness all the time.

My feet are killing me; I am having a severe headache; I feel miserable with this cold and cough; I feel ill; I can't walk any further; this chair is so uncomfortable; please don't expect me to sit on the floor...

How we pamper our bodies from the cradle to the grave! We spend a fortune on clothes and accessories. We are fussy about the kind of food we like to eat. We go out of the way to procure exotic delicacies and expensive tidbits to please our taste buds. We get upset if our sleep is disturbed. We are conscious of every ache and pain in our limbs. We are constantly obsessed with looking good, feeling good, with our physical comforts and with good food. I might even go so far as to say that most of our activities are focused on this obsession with the physical body!

In a beautiful poem on accepting old age with grace, W.B. Yeats writes:

> What youthful mother, a shape upon her lap
> Honey of generation had betrayed,
> And that must sleep, shriek, struggle to escape
> As recollection or the drug decide,
> Would think her Son, did she but see that shape
> With sixty or more winters on its head...

The young mother is fondly holding her newborn baby. In her great love for the child, her labour pains and all the struggles she underwent before she gave birth to him are happily forgotten. It was all worthwhile just to be able to hold this bundle of joy in her hands!

Imagine for a minute, if the young mother could see her newborn babe as a sixty or seventy-year old man, with all the change in appearance and health that old age entails... would she still think her pains worthwhile?

The unanswered question is rhetorical; if the young mother saw a bald/greying/ frail/ decrepit old man instead of the baby with its soft skin and its pink complexion, she would be horrified to realise that this is what will become of her darling boy eventually.

And yet this is what will happen to every baby, to all of us, if we live long enough! Our baby soft skin will wrinkle and shrivel; our thick head of hair will grow sparse and probably leave us bald; very few of us are fortunate enough to keep all our teeth in old age. And we certainly cannot eat and drink as we did in our youth!

Man is mortal; life is fleeting; youth and beauty are transient. We all know this in theoretical abstraction. But we seldom apply it to ourselves in youth. In old age when it has become reality, we are left with a sense of regret!

Anatomy, physiology and neurology can tell us about the body; but even modern psychology has not progressed enough to help us understand the human mind in all its complexity. As for what lies beyond the mind – western science and knowledge have no means to unravel the mysteries of the *atman*. This is where Hindu culture and tradition score over all the rest.

The body is strong; the senses *(indriyas)* are powerful. But the mind *(manas)* is above them. Beyond and higher than the mind is the discriminatory faculty *(buddhi)* that helps us know right from wrong and beyond it all is the *atman* – the Spirit.

This body and its cognitive instruments, the mind and the senses have been given to us with a purpose: that we may evolve towards self-realisation and perfection!

In the Gita, Sri Krishna tells Arjuna:

Nimitramatramsavyasachin

(O, Arjuna, be thou a mere instrument only.)

Ignorance of this great truth brings misery and affliction upon us. Like a caged parrot, we remain imprisoned by the cage of the mind and the senses, confined to the earthly life.

The mind too, can play its games upon us; for good reason or no reason, we get into 'moods'; we are depressed; we are angry; we cannot think clearly; and we allow these feelings to cloud our minds and disrupt our lives.

We are elated when people praise our work; we are delighted when we have our way and we are given prominence over others. The moment we face criticism, the moment we have to take 'No' for an answer, we are 'upset' and lose our balance.

You are Not the Intellect and the Ego

In each of the above instances, it is the ego that has taken a beating!

The intellect, which often is the instigator of the ego, is something which we are all very proud of, especially when we compare ourselves to others. "She is a little slow and dull," we say of people whom we consider to be less smart. These days, we use dismissive terms like "low IQ" and "dumb" which are not merely insulting to our perceived 'inferiors', but actually degrading to us as human beings. Who are we that we judge others to be less 'sharp' or 'quick'? Don't we all go through stages when the mind struggles to grasp concepts? Don't we say at one time or another, "My brain refuses to work; let me tackle this tomorrow."

We work hard to 'sharpen' our intellect; but it can also become dull and slow in understanding the nature of reality.

The causes of human restlessness are not far to seek:

- Constant seeking after sense objects flares up into passion-*kama*.
- When passion is thwarted, there flames up anger – *krodha*.
- Anger leads to loss of reason and sanity – and we pass into a state of delusion – *sanmoha*.

- In this state of delusion, we lose our memory – *smriti*. We lose the memory of our Guru's *upadesh*, the memory of our life's great ideals.
- Losing this memory, we also lose the power of discrimination; we lose reason – *buddhi*.

Let me sum up, in the words of Gurudev Sadhu Vaswani:

When the mind is bewildered, confused, you forget the lesson of experience; that is loss of memory. Forgetting experience, you lose discrimination. Losing discrimination, you miss the purpose of life. It is the real loss of man himself.

Just consider this: we actually spend more than one half of our lives free from the domination of these three false selves, namely the mind, the senses and the ego: they cease to matter to us when we are in the state of sleep.

In other words, we are not the intellect or the ego!

Our sages tell us that Ego or *ahamkara,* is the nucleus of man's mental and intellectual process. It is easy to transcend the body and the mind; it is easy to discipline the senses; it is extremely difficult to transcend the ego!

According to Hindu philosophy, as enunciated in the Gita, we can be under the domination of three types of ego: *tamasic* ego, *rajasicego* and *sattvic* ego. *Tamasic ego* is gross and makes us slaves of base emotions like anger, greed, envy, jealousy and lust. *Rajasic* ego leads us to value our pride, vanity, power and possessions above all else. *Sattvic* ego is better than the rest; it leads us to explore the questions we have raised again and again: who am I? What is the nature of my true self? It also leads us to seek association with good people and urges us to find a guru. *Sattvic* ego dominates a pure mind and a cleansed intellect. It can successfully lead you to transcend the ego-self and understand the true nature of the *atman*.

This transcendence is not easy! *Kastarati Kastarati, Kastarati Mayam...* says Sage *Narada* in his *Bhakti Sutra:* "He who crosses over, crosses over, crosses over Maya..." The thrice repeated term stresses the fact that this cross-over is not easy! Tied down by *maya,* led by *maya*, how we have whirled in the cycle of birth and death! But the moment we cut ourselves off from identification with the body, the moment we cross over *maya,* we realise our oneness with the Self, and we move towards emancipation – *jivanmukti.*

In the simplest terms, spirituality is the aspiration, the genuine effort to know our true self. It begins with the realisation that we are not the bodies we wear; that this materialistic world we live in, cannot satisfy our deepest aspirations; that our unquenchable desire for wealth and power cannot really give us the joy and peace that we truly crave…

Finding your soul – that is the essence of self-knowledge. And as we attempt to rediscover, reassert our true identity, we begin to realise the spiritual dimension that is unique to us.

The quest for self-knowledge adds value to human life; it is an attitude to life; an approach to the purpose of existence.

Let me sum up what I have said earlier: all of us subsist on a physical plane; we cannot do without those basic needs – *roti, kapda aur makaan* as they are called – food, clothing and shelter. However, all of us have desires that go beyond these needs; we crave for more wealth, more possessions, more acquisitions; but the intelligent ones among us know that wealth and possessions cannot really make us happy. We live by our passions; beyond what we crave passionately, we live by our own sets of morals and values; we look to higher ideals; we are fascinated by the rare moments in our life when we are filled with awe, wonder and a sense of mystery…feelings, moods, aspirations that send our spirits soaring…

We all know that none of these finer feelings can be captured by a materialistic way of life!

In the past, the distinction between spirituality and the workaday world was so sharp that people turned their back on one to face the other squarely. They renounced the world and worldly activities to contemplate on the higher things of life. But today, the boundaries have softened.

What I mean about the blurring of boundaries is that all of us, laymen and women, students and working professionals, businessmen and managers, young and old are deeply concerned about their holistic growth as human beings. Everybody is concerned about their inner life; everyone craves for a sense of peace and harmony that is central to their being. We may not want to renounce the world to find that elusive peace; but we are ready and willing to spend some time focusing our attention on the rich interior world that is within us.

We must understand this clearly: transcending the ego is not a state of self-annihilation: it is a state of bliss because we realise our identification with the entire universe, with the Divinity that animates all creation. We realise that we are not the limited, weak, miserable creatures that we took ourselves to be, crawling between birth and death.

Swami Vivekananda tells us:

The essence of Vedanta is: *Atam Brahmasmi: Tat Twam Asi*. That art thou! You are essentially Divine. Vedanta recognises no sin; it recognises only error. And the greatest error, it says, is to think that you are weak, that you are a sinner, a miserable creature...

There is no room in the Hindu way of life for such defeatism or negative thinking!

Tat Twam Asi! That art thou!

———————◇◇◇◇◇◇▷◁◆▶◁◇◇◇◇◇———————

Mano buddhya-hankarachittaninaham
Na cha shrotrajihve, na cha ghrananetre
Na cha vyomabhumirnatejonavayuhu
Chidananda rupah shivoham shivoham

I am not the mind, intellect, thought, ego, or some form of the supreme being; I neither have ears, nor tongue and I neither have nostrils, nor eyes; I am not the sky, earth, light or the wind; I am the fortunate, joyful, Supreme Being who is the very emblem of truth, knowledge and eternal bliss.

I am consciousness and bliss. I am Shiva, I am Shiva.

- Adi Shankara

———————◇◇◇◇◇◇▷◁◆▶◁◇◇◇◇◇———————

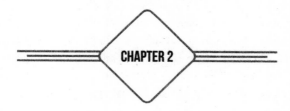

CHAPTER 2

EGO — IS IT GOOD OR BAD?

Leave the ego; or else everyone will leave you.

- Anonymous

Detachment from the Ego

The Yoga Vashishta tells us the story of king who bore the name Sikhidhwaja, who was "replete with the goodness of charity and all other virtues, and preserved that silence which avoids the discord born of words". He had cultivated mental and physical discipline and especially delighted in doing good to others. The partner of his marriage was Chudala, a remarkable princess from Saurashtra, who was born through Tapas. Not in the space of the whole world could we find one to compare with her in her imperishable virtue.

And the couple lived together in perfect happiness with their two minds interblended, enjoying the virtuous life of the *grihastashrama* (married state), performing all actions without the least difference of opinion, helping each other in every way possible. But as the years rolled on and their youth was left behind, their thoughts turned away from the world and they began to cherish higher aspirations. They both realised that it was only *mukti,* Liberation from the endless cycle of birth and death which would give them true happiness.

Having arrived at this conclusion, both of them began to pursue the goal in their own way. They spent time in the company of wise and holy men; they read the scriptures together. In short, they lived their life in the way of practical spirituality, fulfilling their worldly duties and obligations, while keeping their mind steadily on the desired goal of Liberation.

Queen Chudala chose the way of self-enquiry. Going deep within herself, she sought true knowledge of the self. Her steadfast and persistent enquiry gave her the powers of discrimination and detachment (*viveka* and *vairagya*). Coming thus to the conclusion that re-birth cannot be avoided except through *Atma-Gnana* (knowledge of the spirit) alone, she soon realised that the body-mind complex, the senses, the mind and their cognizing powers had to be purified, so that the ego *(ahamkara)* could be mastered. Having realised this, she delved deeper and deeper into the self through meditation until she attained *atma gnana* or true knowledge of the self. She had attained the state of a *jeevanmukta* in this life. This attainment gave her a radiance, a spiritual effulgence that made her glow with the spirit of *sat chit ananda.*

The King noticed this wonderful transformation in his wife and said to her playfully, "Dearest one, won't you reveal to me the secret of your beautiful radiance? How is it that you appear like a being from *devaloka,* here on earth? What is it that suffuses you with that inner glow that radiates so powerfully?"

Quite truthfully, the queen confessed to her husband, "This is my secret, O, Beloved of my heart. I have attained *atma gnana* – knowledge of the Self. I dwell here on earth for the remainder of my life. But nothing binds me to this state. For I know I am That which is beyond this world of illusion."

The King laughed aloud. "I pity you dearest," he said, "that you should so deceive yourself. You are after all a woman, the weaker vessel. You live a life of luxury in the palace as my queen. How can you even talk of self-realisation here? Great gnanis and *tapasvis* have gone through severe austerities and penances to attain the state you speak of. You must know what is true renunciation before you make such tall claims."

Having thus dismissed his wife's words, the king went about his tasks as usual. Chudala saw that her words had failed to convince him and decided to maintain a discreet silence on the issue. But the fact of the matter was that she had attained to *taatwa gnana* (true knowledge) and this gave her a sense of detachment that enabled her to feel fully the state of bliss, even while she lived her worldly life.

But the king grew increasingly troubled with his failure to attain self-realisation. Believing firmly that his royal life and regal duties could only be impediments on the path, he decided to renounce worldly life and retire to the *tapobana,* the forest of meditation, to seek the truth there in the manner of all great ascetics and renunciates. He knew that his people loved him and that Chudala herself was utterly devoted to him, and would not hear of his retirement. So one fine day, he left the palace in stealth and sought the confines of a faraway forest. Here he built himself a *kutiya.* His only possessions were his *kamandalu,* a rod and a string of *rudraksha* beads. Here in the deep dark woods, he lived a life of penance and sought the elusive truth which his soul aspired to. He undertook the hardest forms of penance; he fasted and stayed awake and deprived himself of the most basic necessities that could keep a man in bare existence. He became weak and emaciated, reduced to a bag of bones. But, alas, enlightenment was nowhere in sight!

In her state of self-realisation, Queen Chudala perceived through her *gnana drishti* (inner vision) the state of her beloved Lord. She was filled with compassion for his plight and she longed to show him the way to the truth. But she knew that the King was so stubborn that he would not accept her words. With her yogic powers, she went to the forest where he lived, taking her astral form. How she grieved to see his wasted, emaciated form! She knew that such harsh penance was just a waste of time in the path of self-realisation. The king had merely run away from the world and his responsibilities in life.

The king opened his eyes. In a trice, Chudala assumed the form of a young Brahmin, a *tejaswi* (radiant one) who stood before the king as he awoke from a trance.

Instinctively, the king stood up at the sight of the young Brahmin and folded his hands in a gesture of respect. Chudala returned the greeting. She introduced herself as Kumbha Muni, a young sage, and enquired as to what the king was doing here. The King replied that he had renounced the world and was living in the forest in pursuit of truth.

"You do not seem to have renounced anything!" exclaimed the young sage. "I have come here to tell you that what you are doing is not true *sadhana.*"

"How can you say that?" exclaimed the king in anguish. "I have renounced my royal palace, my life of luxury, my kingdom and my virtuous, beautiful wife, to come here and practise my austerities. If this is not renunciation, pray tell me what else I should give up!"

"This is not true renunciation," repeated the young Brahmin. "You are not aware of the meaning of renunciation."

Deeply disturbed by these words, the king burnt his *kutiya;* he threw away his *kamandalu,* his rod and his *rudraksha beads* into the flowing river. "Now, I own nothing, I have nothing," he cried. "Is this not renunciation?"

The sage shook his head in negation.

Incensed by this heartless denial, the king climbed up to the top of a tall tree and readied to throw himself down from that great height. "Behold, young sage," he announced, "I throw my life away to prove to you that I have renounced everything."

"You can throw away only your perishable body, O, King," laughed the young sage. "How will that help you? The body is but an instrument you have brought with you in this life to help you evolve and progress on the path. What will you attain when you throw it away? You will only reap the terrible consequences of *aatma hatya,* or suicide. You will have to go through the misery of endless lives before you can be free of this terrible sin!"

The king sank into deep despair. He fell at the feet of the Brahmin and begged him, "Sire! I humbly beseech you to accept me as your disciple. Show me the way to self-realisation. Show me the way of truth, the *tattwa gnana.*"

"O, King, true renunciation is renunciation of the ego, that *ahamkara* which feeds on the illusion that you are the doer and that you will reap the fruits of your actions. Real renunciation consists in renouncing egoism, in renouncing the cravings and the desires, in renouncing the intellect that makes you identify yourself with the perishable body, that foolishly mistakes the body to be the soul. This ego you will have to renounce and only that constitutes real renunciation."

The King was amazed to hear these words and begged the sage to be his *Acharya* and instruct him in spiritual matters.

"If you pour oil on water, the two can never mix," the sage explained to him kindly. "And so it is with the spiritual and the material world. The objects of the senses can never touch the spirit because materialism can never contaminate the spirit. When you identify yourself with the material reality of this world, you suffer. Realise that you are That, and the sorrows and joys of this world will never touch you."

The Light of truth dawned on the King and then and there, he went into a state of deep *Samadhi.* He had at last attained to the truth he was seeking.

When he opened his eyes at long last, Chudala stood before him. He was overjoyed to see her. Together, they returned to the kingdom and led a righteous life, in the world and yet detached from the world in spirit. At the end of their earthly lives, they attained to Liberation, as they had always wanted.

Identifying the Ego

If you were to trace the history of the word, you will come to know that in the original Latin, the word "ego" meant self, or identity.

According to Sigmund Freud, the ego is not a part of the brain but a function of the mind. It is said that Freud first used the term "ego" to mean a sense of self, but later revised it to mean "a set of psychic functions such as judgement, tolerance, reality testing, control, planning, defense, synthesis of information, intellectual functioning, and memory." Freud taught that the ego actually "attempts to mediate between *id* and reality", and thus serves a very useful function.

In modern parlance, ego has come to mean something else! It is an exaggerated sense of self-importance; an inflated feeling of pride in one's (imagined) superiority over others. When egoism manifests itself in outward behaviour, it becomes arrogance: "Overbearing pride evidenced by a superior manner toward inferiors," to quote a widely accepted definition.

There is also a slightly more positive meaning attributed to the ego: which is simply a sense of one's own identity, an appropriate sense of self-esteem. Ego is also the opinion you have about yourself. Some of you may be surprised to know that the following terms are used as synonyms for ego: self-esteem, self-regard, pride in oneself/one's abilities, faith in oneself, dignity, morale, self-confidence, confidence, self-assurance, and self-respect.

So let us raise the question: is ego good or bad for you?

Someone had this to say of the ego: the ego is what you think you are; it is what you make yourself out to be. It may be 'false' but it is as false as the reflection you see of your face in the mirror; that is the only 'you' you will ever know. May be we are confused about our identity; maybe we really do not know the true self that we are; may be the 'I' changes from moment to moment, mood to mood. But the sense of 'I'ness is always there!

Many experts tell us that ego is necessary to our survival in so far as facing challenges, tough situations and crises in life are concerned. After all, what helps us to come out of depression and failure? The feeling that I-will-not-allow-myself-to-be-crushed. When you have to fight against odds, when you have to battle adversities, the ego is your greatest support. Personal care and hygiene, doing well in your studies or excelling in your business, working for better recognition and appreciation, even achievement orientation are all, to a certain extent, motivated by the ego.

In that wonderful story of "The Old Man and the Sea", we have the memorable character of the old and frail fisherman, Santiago. Alone, he battles with a giant fish which he has actually hooked and caught, but which takes control of him and his small skiff and pulls the boat at its will. The old man is desperately trying to hold on to the fishing line so that he may save himself; he is fighting against the might of the huge fish; nevertheless, he is filled with deep admiration for the fish, whom he regards as his brother in suffering, struggle and pain. Finally, he manages to kill the fish with his harpoon and sets sail for home. But the fish, which is too big to be carried in the small skiff, and which is lashed to the outside of the boat, is attacked by giant sharks which devour the entire carcass, leaving only the head, tail and skeleton. There is nothing for the old man to sell; no catch to offer. But the skeletal remains of the fish stands as mute testimony to his philosophy: man may be destroyed, but not defeated. Effort may motivate a man to greatness.

One way of looking at higher awareness is to regard it as 'ego-expansion'. For what is it but expansion of the self to become aware of the *mahavakya, Aham Brahmasmi* or *Sohum!* If we were not capable of realising that we are not the limited beings, the petty selves that we take ourselves to be, we would be trapped in our lowest self! Perhaps what is called for here is ego transcendence, rather than ego-expansion!

It also takes the highest form of ego-consciousness to assert the truth that all of us are princes and princesses, loving children of God, the King of kings. It takes a strong sense of the self to assert that as princes and princesses, there are certain things that we must never stoop to do!

Many psychologists argue that all work, all effort, all striving towards excellence is ego-driven. The very feeling that I must do my best, I must put my best foot forward is derived from a strong sense of self-worth. As long as this effort is not derogatory to others' wellbeing, ego is not a bad thing at all! What I am trying to say is that your self-impelled, self-fulfilling efforts can be aligned with selfless goals, if you are working for a common good!

Let me give you an example. The image of athletes running the 100 m. race is one with which we are all familiar. It is only by harnessing the ego to achieve victory that men and women have shattered records and won laurels in the Olympics. Their ego has helped them cultivate self-discipline, hard work and commitment to the cause and they 'come out on top' through a tremendous effort of the will.

And we all know the image of victory in such a race: the winning athlete or sports person is handed his or her national flag and he or she takes a victory lap as it is called, around the stadium, with spectators cheering them. The flag is a symbol of patriotism, which is also an expansion of one's ego sense– the feeling which tells us that we are proud to be Indian, American or Chinese!

The ego then, is not all bad, when it is used in the right direction, spent in the right cause. It is like the familiar story of the belly, which we are all familiar with. If you recall, all the different parts of the body once refused to work, saying that they were tired of serving the stomach. The legs said, "What is the use of running about from morning till night, merely to find food enough to fill the stomach? There's nothing in it for us."

"We won't work for that lazy stomach either!" said the hands and arms. "Legs, if, you'll keep still, we won't move either."

"We too, are fed up," said the teeth. "We go grinding, grinding , grinding, all day long. And it's all in aid of the belly. Let the stomach do its own dirty work hereafter."

Soon, all the parts of the body joined the vociferous chorus. Each and every limb had the same complaint to make about the stomach, and all agreed that they would not work anymore to satisfy its wants. The legs stopped walking, the hands and arms stopped working, the teeth did not grind any more, and the empty stomach clamored in vain for its daily supply of food.

All the limbs were delighted at first with their rest, and, when the empty stomach called for something to eat, they merely laughed. Their fun did not last very long, however, because the stomach, weak for want of food, soon ceased its cries. Then, after a while, the hands and arms and legs grew so weak that they could not move. The body fell down weak and emaciated for lack of nutrition. They realised that the stomach, which was left unfed, could no longer supply the rest of the body with strength to live.

When your ego creates resistance to others' wellbeing, or if you imagine that you are forced to work for their benefit, and decide to become selfish, you are harming your own interests.

People who write books and self-help manuals, people who work to motivate others, people who mobilise groups to protect the environment are not just feeding their own ego. They are helping others; and in the process, they are also enhancing their own self-esteem.

Creativity is also associated with ego. It is their belief in their talents and in themselves that enables artists to create masterpieces. They achieve excellence for themselves and they make the world richer with their artistic contributions.

Such people have become involved with something larger than themselves. In a sense, their ego has served a useful purpose for themselves and the rest of humanity.

Some people refer to negative and positive ego. We saw that the ego creates a sense of the self, a sense of identity for each of us. It creates that subtle sense of separation between "me" and "others". When this sense of "me" or "I" assumes extravagant proportions, it becomes arrogance, pride, vanity and excessive egoism. At the other extreme, when it is defeated and thwarted and frustrated in its ambitions and desires, it leads to self-pity, victim syndrome and paranoia.

I would say that the sense of separation, the sense of exclusion and isolation is what makes the ego a negative force. The stronger and more selfish the ego, the greater the sense of separation and the 'disconnect' that exists between us and others. When we become aware that as individual entities we are not apart from the Universe, but an intrinsic part of a larger whole, then the sense of separation ceases to exist, and our personal good and our personal goals are in tune with the common good and the common goals of all humanity. In this state, the ego is a source of light; it ceases to weigh heavily on us; it becomes positive.

The negative ego – i.e. excessive desire, insatiable craving and selfish drive– are the cause of all human unhappiness. Experts tell us that the negative ego is constantly in a state of restlessness. It always imagines that there is a treasure of happiness and fulfillment somewhere out there, and it can never feel fulfilled until this treasure is attained. Unfortunately, this elusive treasure is often a petty, selfish personal goal like money, wealth or personal power. The negative ego labours under this delusion that it is only the attainment of this personal goal that can make it truly happy. Alas, such happiness is at best transient and fleeting. It may bring temporary satiation of desire, but the old restlessness and unhappiness will return to haunt us!

We can become servants of our ego, constantly striving to satisfy its many cravings and urges, making ourselves miserable everytime the ego is defeated and feeling vulnerable because the ego suffers massive wounds and hurts. Or we can become masters of the ego, not controllers and mangers, but whole human beings capable of transcending the ego, letting it go and asserting our identity as larger, whole beings.

When I say 'let go' I do not mean that literally; I mean, stop fueling and feeding the ego constantly. Realise that you are much larger than the ego and that it cannot hamper the free flow of your life energy. When you free yourself from the pull of the ego, it is as if you are released from prison! You then realise that life is larger than the ego and has a greater purpose than mere ego-gratification!

Be in the world, but not of the world. Hence cultivate detachment. Attachment to worldly forms or objects distances us from the Reality. He who is detached, is not enamoured by worldly wealth, nor is he a slave to lust. Sure, there are people who are indifferent to their wealth, family, and status, but some of them are attached to their business, profession, research, art or their institutions. A true pilgrim on the path is the one who has no attachment to any kind of worldly affairs. He lives in the world, but is not attached to the world; being detached, he is able to realise God!

Gurudev Sadhu Vaswani said to us: "Everyone lives amidst the activities of this world, everyone has to act and do one's duty. We must only act with understanding without getting attached to this world of *maya*. O pilgrim, grow in your spiritual strength, in this journey of the physical body. O pilgrim, do not get attached."

The last line is worth all our attention and should be remembered.

We have worn this physical garb to come on this planet earth. We are not the gross physical bodies we wear. The body is only a garment. This body is given to us to perform acts of worldly duties. It is through the physical body that we gather experiences which help our souls to evolve. In reality, what you regard as your 'self' is not the 'body' – the body is perishable. You are the 'soul', which is imperishable, and eternal.

No one has ever seen the face of ego. It is like a ghost that we accept as a controlling influence in our lives. I look upon the ego as nothing more than an idea that each of us has about ourselves. The ego is only an illusion, but a very influential one. Letting the ego-illusion become your identity can prevent you from knowing your true self. Ego, the false idea of believing that you are what you have or what you do, is a backwards way of assessing and living life.

Dr. Wayne W. Dyer

CHAPTER 3

WHEN THE EGO SPELLS TROUBLE - FLAWS OF MASSIVE EGO

The ego is not master in its own house.

- Sigmund Freud

King Hugo's Huge Ego

"King Hugo's Huge Ego" is a clever, witty and funny story by author and illustrator, Chris Van Dusen. In its time, it became a children's classic; but adults can learn from it too!

King Hugo is one tiny monarch with a very large Napoleon complex. Hugo rules the land with an iron fist and a rather bloated sense of self; his ego is head and shoulders above his three foot three stature.

"Yes, Hugo was a cocky king - as boastful as could be. To him, no other person was as wonderful as he."

King Hugo makes sure his subjects bow to him whenever he passes (wouldn't want them to be taller!), and they are treated every Friday morning to his "Speech of Adoration". What's the subject of that adoration? You guessed it; it's Hugo!

One day, while riding in his coach, he encounters a peasant girl who will not get out of his way or bow to him, so Hugo has his coachman bump her right off the road. What he doesn't know is that the peasant, Tessa, is a sorceress. Tessa proceeds to put a spell on Hugo that makes his head grow larger every time he boasts about himself (very similar to what happens to Pinocchio's nose when he tells a lie), until it is hilariously large. Finally, it just becomes too big to be supported by his tiny, little body! Hugo returns to Tessa, who explains her spell and why she did it. King Hugo sees the errors of his ways and ends up Tessa's husband and becomes a much kinder, humbler king. All's well that ends well.

Dangers of a swollen head

We often talk of a swollen head, a massive ego and pompous arrogance. In the above story, all of it becomes literal! The ego can make you its slave, if you do not learn to be its Master!

Brian Jones, a Stanford-trained neuroscientist says, "The ego is not'a thing' like your ribs, your feet, or your prefrontal cortex. Rather, the ego is reflective of an underlying bio-chemical state of stress and insecurity in our perceived-as-threatening dog-eat-dog world. Biologically, the ego and our personality, thoughts and emotions are really run by the energy of our autonomic nervous system, which is either in a stressed, ego-centered, fearful state called the Sympathetic Response, or a secure, relaxed state called the Parasympathetic Response."

The ego, in its positive state, uncontaminated by selfishness, can give us determination and confidence as well as a clear sense of purpose; but in a negative state, when it is dominated by selfish impulses, it can give us a false sense of ourselves and lead us on to think that we are the greatest in the world, and no one else really matters.

The ego becomes poisonous when it is coupled with power and authority. Thus we have certain types of politicians, certain types of stars and celebrities and even certain types of leaders and executives, who begin to think that they are the alpha and omega of existence, and that the entire population of the world exists to love and admire them and carry out their bidding. They live in the delusion that they are very special and their needs and wants must take precedence over everyone else's.

I said certain politicians and certain celebrities... because all of them are NOT devoured by the ego. It has been our good fortune to come across many great leaders and celebrities at the Sadhu Vaswani Mission who were the very pictures of modesty and good nature.

Let me say this again: the ego is essential to our survival and our achievements. Experts tell us that there would be no progress, no evolution to higher forms of awareness, if we were not impelled by the motivation, the drive to reach beyond our grasp. It is only when the ego begins to dominate, overpower the self that problems are created.

A genuine leader once said to me that being powerful means that one is strong in the power of loving kindness! For true power is never corrosive or control-seeking; it is about offering everyone the best help and service that you are capable of!

Alas, for many of us, I'm afraid, the ego is unconquerable. Man has conquered space; man has conquered the sky; man has controlled even the courses of the rivers and the growth of the great forests – but man has not found it easy to control or conquer the ego.

It is the presence of unconscious *vasanas* (subtle desires) in the mind which give rise to ego. Most of our human interactions are based on the ego. In fact, for the vast majority of the people, their ego is their identity. When people are disgruntled or disappointed, their ego begins to rise like high fever. They try to assert themselves, to assert their self-will, their ego. Little do they realise that ego only blocks the flow of energy and power into their lives!

For many of us, our life on earth is nothing more than a parade of ego-desires. As the ego changes, our desires change as well. The little child craves toys; the young boy wants computer games and gadgets; the young man chases after fast cars and girls; the grown-up man chases wealth and power. And so we hanker after shadow shapes, fondly imagining that fulfilling the ego desires will make us happy.

From birth to birth, from one life to another, the ego changes its shape and form like a cloud – the cloud that hides the sun, the source of light, the sense of our real identity.

Identification with the body, egoism and ignorance of the true nature of the self – these three are identified by sages as the cause of all human suffering.

The danger of an excessive ego is beautifully brought out in this simple fable from our ancient legends. A frog asked two geese to take him south with them. At first they resisted; they didn't see how it could be done. Finally, the frog suggested that the two geese hold a stick in their beaks and that he would hold on to it with his mouth.

So off the unlikely threesome went, flying southward over the countryside. It was really quite a sight. People looked up and expressed great admiration for this demonstration of creative teamwork.

Someone said, "It's wonderful! Who was so clever to discover such a fine way to travel?" Whereupon the frog opened his mouth and said, "It was I," and promptly plummeted to his death.

A consultant on corporate affairs once said to me that ego has also been the cause of several companies 'going under' as he put it. "Excessive ego is like a runaway train, killing everyone and everything in its path," he observed. After all, excessive ego makes you feel that you have nothing to learn – not even from your own or others' mistakes; it makes you imagine that there is nothing anyone can ever teach you. And when ego closes your mind thus, you are in danger of stagnation, in a state of illusion!

"Hypocrisy, pride, self-conceit, wrath, arrogance and ignorance belong, O Partha, to him who is born to the heritage of the demons," Sri Krishna tells Arjuna, in the Gita. Truly, an inflated ego can be diabolical in the havoc it wreaks.

The *Tao Te Ching* tells us: "The best athlete wants his opponent at his best. The best general enters the mind of his enemy. The best businessman serves the communal good. The best leader follows the will of the people. All of them embody the virtue of non-competition. Not that they don't love to compete, but they do it in the spirit of play. In this they are like children and in harmony with the Tao."

In this age when competition is equated with the killer instinct, we will do well to remember these words! "Win at all costs" or "It's ok if I lose one eye, as long as my opponent loses both his eyes," is a deadly attitude fuelled by poisonous ego!

Rightly has it been said: "Ego has a voracious appetite, the more you feed it, the hungrier it gets."

It is not without reason that Ravana is regarded as the arch symbol of excessive ego in Hindu mythology. You have heard of the story: chop off one head and another appears in its place. Some scholars say that the ten heads represent ten different forms of evil: *ahankar* (ego), *krodh* (anger), *alasya* (laze), *lobha* (greed), *kama* (lust), *aparigraha* (covetousness), *hinsa* (violence), *moha* (attachment), *madha* (lustful passion), and *droha* (betrayal). Thus, different people have different interpretations about his ten heads.

It is said that Ravana belonged to a family of *bhaktas*. But he became so powerful and egoistic that he felt he was greater than the Gods. In his arrogance, and blind egoism, he inserted his toes beneath Mount Kailash, the abode of Lord Shiva, with the intention of overturning the mountain from its base. Incensed with his arrogance, Lord Shiva, sitting in his yogic posture, put the slightest pressure on the mountain top with his foot. Ravana's toes were almost crushed beneath the weight of the mountain and he endured the greatest pain. Realising his mistake, he started the harshest form of penance to appease Lord Shiva. His *tapsya* continued for years together, until Shiva forgave him and blessed him with unique weapons. Ravana became a Shiva *bhakta* for life. Sadly, that did not stop his ego-trip!

Lord Shiva also granted Ravana the special boon that he could not be killed or defeated by gods, *rakshasas* or *yakshas*. In his arrogance, he believed that no one else could ever be his match; thus he ignored *nara* (man) and *vanara* (monkey) who were not included as potential rivals. As we know, Lord Vishnu took on the *avatara* of a man, Rama, and killed Ravana with the help of the *vanarasena* (army of monkeys)

Ravana symbolizes all those evils that we indulge in, if only to a lesser extent. We seek pleasure most of the time. We become addicted to bad habits even when we know that they are bad for us. We live for the pleasure of self-indulgence. We arrogantly assume that we can master Nature (just as Ravana decided to abduct Sita Mata). Alas, we become blind to the great Law of *karma* when we pursue carnal pleasures. Worst of all, we think nothing, nobody can touch us. Our arrogance becomes our delusion of invincibility and our ultimate folly!

When I said that Ravana's evils were in all of us, I dare say some of you were offended! But the point I am trying to make is this – that when we allow ourselves to be guided by ego and excessive desire, we are seeking our own ruin!

Ravana is alive! So who are we burning every year?

On Dussera /Vijayadashami every year, we burn the effigy of Ravana. There is a deeper meaning behind this action or ritual. The celebration, arrangements, processions and rituals of Ram-Leela have become commercial, and at times political, and a lot of hoopla goes around it. In that, we seem to have lost the real meaning behind it...

Ravana is the personification of vices while Sri Rama is the embodiment of virtues. Ravana, Kansa, Putna, Shishupal and Duryodhana, represent the life of impurity, egoism, self-centeredness and covetousness. Rama and Ravana are both living within us. When we live a pure life in thought, words and deeds, we express Rama within us but when we live in vain ego, pride, covetousness, and hypocrisy, we are expressing Ravana. So, whenever we see these vices being expressed anywhere by anyone, know that Ravana is very much alive. Burning an effigy is symbolic of getting rid of egoism, pride, hypocrisy and other vices from our daily living.

- Swami Adhyatmananda

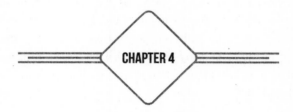

CHAPTER 4

HOW EGO CAN ENDANGER RELATIONSHIPS

Relationships never die a natural death…They are murdered by Ego, Attitude and Ignorance…

- Anonymous

Remembering Urmila

How many of us remember Urmila from the Ramayana?

Most of us will have to jog our memories a bit and then say, "She was the wife of Lakshmana, wasn't she?"

Indeed, Urmila was the wife of Lakshmana, the daughter of King Janaka and Queen Sunayana, and the younger sister of Princess Sita. The sisters were given away in marriage along with their cousins, Mandavi and Shrutakirti to the four sons of King Dasharata. Urmila comes into prominence for a very brief while in the story; when Lakshmana decides to accompany his brother and sister-in-law to the forest on their fourteen year exile, Urmila asks to go with him; her reasoning is irrefutable: if Sita considers it right to accompany her husband wherever he goes, doesn't the same rule apply to Urmila too? Is it not her duty to be with Lakshmana wherever he may be?

I am sure Lakshmana must have been taken aback by the force of the argument. But he requests his wife to stay behind in Ayodhya and carry out his filial responsibilities to his parents. Urmila agrees, albeit reluctantly. She is left behind, to suffer the pangs of separation from her beloved husband for fourteen long years.

If truth were to be told, Maharishi Valmiki tells us very little about Urmila, although he eulogises her sacrifice and selflessness. This has led to a lot of hard feelings amongst feminist scholars, who claim that Urmila is the most neglected character in the Ramayana; that it is she, and not Sita who is the epitome of the ideal wife.

Our native and folk versions of the Ramayana, especially in South India, give a great deal of prominence to this selfless heroine who helps to bring out the best in her husband. *Urmila Devi Nidra* (Urmila's Sleep) is one of the most famous ballads in Telugu Literature. The well-known Hindi poet, Maithili Sharan Gupta too, makes her the heroine of his version of the Ramayana called *Saket.*

What is so special about this unseen, almost unheard heroine that so many writers and readers are fascinated by her story? As one among four princesses who married Dasharata's sons, she has a very minor role to play.

She asks to accompany her husband to the forest; but when he requests her to stay behind and look after his ageing parents, she consents; and stoically resigns herself to long years of loneliness and silent anguish.

It is said that on the first night of their exile to the forest, Sri Rama and Sita slept on the bare earth underneath a tree, and Lakshmana stood guard to protect them. His thoughts were all focused on the plight of his beloved brother, born to be King, but forced to live the life of an ascetic now; and the divine princess who was to have been his royal consort, but now enduring exile and hardship with him. Lakshmana pledged to himself that he would guard them with his heart and soul and ensure that no harm came to them. For a moment, his thoughts went out to his wife Urmila. How desperately she had pleaded with him to let him join her! But he had been firm; he had pointed out to her that his life's mission, the purpose of his birth was to serve his brother; now, when they faced the prospect of fourteen years in the wild, untamed forests, he would need to have all his wits about him in order to protect Rama and Sita; if Urmila went with them, she would only be a source of distraction for him…

Urmila had not uttered a word in protest; she had only looked at him with tear-filled eyes and nodded her consent…

Looking back on that moment, Lakshmana blessed his dear wife in gratitude and love; truly, she had helped him fulfill the purpose of his life.

At that moment, the Goddess of sleep, Nidradevi, appeared before him. The moment he saw the goddess, Lakshmana felt his vision blurring and his sharp mental processes slowing down. The goddess said to him, "O, Prince! What you wish to do goes against the laws of Nature. Consider this: for almost one half of their lifetime, human beings are under my sway, for that is the nature of their existence. When I hold sway over you, how would you protect your beloved brother and his wife?"

Lakshmana realised the effect that sleep could have over him, and begged the goddess to free him from her rule for fourteen years, until Rama and Sita were safely back in Ayodhya.

"Your request is indeed worthy of a devoted brother," said the goddess. "I am willing to forego my control over you for fourteen years, during which you shall remain sleepless without any adverse effects on you.

But you must point out someone who is willing to take on your share of sleep during those fourteen years."

Without a moment's hesitation, Lakshmana begged Nidradevi to approach his wife Urmila. When Urmila heard the goddess, she said to her humbly, "The only boon I ask of you is that my husband should ever, ever remain steadfast and unswerving in his service and dedication to his brother. I am prepared to take on any condition you impose on me to help him achieve his goal."

And so, the story goes, Urmila remained asleep for fourteen long years, taking on her husband's 'burden' of sleep, while Lakshmana remained sleepless, guarding his beloved brother with his life. There was another benefit from this; Indrajeet, Ravana's son, had obtained a boon that he could only be vanquished by one who had not slept a wink for fourteen years. Urmila's sacrifice and Nidradevi's boon helped Lakshmana fulfill this condition and thus he became the hero who was able to vanquish the invincible Indrajeet in battle!

At the end of fourteen years, when Rama was crowned King of Ayodhya, Lakshmana felt himself being overpowered by sleep; as he slipped into slumber, Urmila came awake, and beheld the blessed sight of Sri Rama's coronation!

Keep Ego out of your Relationships

I am sure that my readers are too intelligent to need footnotes for this story; but I crave the indulgence of a few comments. The 'sleep' imposed on Urmila is obviously metaphorical; it refers to the state of suspended animation or the death-in-life situation endured by a loving wife who is physically separated from her husband. This may not appeal to some of our modern ideas of independence and equality in marriage! But the fact remains that Urmila's understanding nature, her selflessness, her patience and her silent sacrifice are commendable qualities that nurture a vital relationship.

We no longer value a woman who lives for her husband or her children; we insist that there is more to a woman than family and relationships. But I think no woman would willingly sacrifice her relationships for the sake of achieving career goals or professional success! For that matter, no man would wish to do that either. Ideally, we would want to have it all: professional success, personal fulfillment and rewarding relationships within and outside the family!

The old proverb stating that there is a woman behind every successful man has now become gender-sensitive, and we acknowledge that there is an understanding man, indeed an understanding family, including a sweet natured and helpful mother-in-law (mother-in-love, as I like to call her), behind every successful woman! All our most successful women would agree that they would not have got to where they were, without the love and support of their family.

The wife of a successful executive or businessman puts aside her selfish or personal claims upon his time; she takes on his responsibilities at home and gives him the space to succeed. Equally, an understanding husband encourages his wife's aspirations and special talents and gives her the kind of environment where she can succeed. If ego intervenes in such relationships, everyone loses!

Urmila did not ask Lakshmana, "If Sita can go with Rama, why can't I go with you?" She did not accuse him of putting her second (or possibly third) after his brother and his parents. If she had, she would have been another Kaikeyi, insisting on her rights and her priorities and her wishes!

Let me hasten to add, this kind of understanding and support are not the prerogative of the high and mighty, the educated and the privileged classes! Among our urban middle class families and the less sophisticated rural families, there are countless men and women who are content to make adjustments, to give-and-take to make their family life happy. Unfortunately, there are others who refuse to do this; their ego will not let them give anything; they only want to take; and this cannot make any relationship successful; when ego enters, relationships become warships!

Young wives do not want to 'share' their husbands' time and love with his parents; mothers and fathers are at times resentful of being babysitters for their grandchildren; sons and daughters do not like their parents to 'interfere' in their personal lives. "I need my privacy,"; "I need my space," is the constant refrain we hear these days. "Thus far and no further," is an unwritten, unspoken law that we impose on our loved ones.

It is not just family relationships that suffer on account of our ego; as I often tell my friends, the greatest famine in the world today is the famine of understanding. No two people seem to understand each other these days! Therefore, misunderstandings abound in our lives. There is misunderstanding in our homes, our clubs, our schools, colleges, universities, corporations and organizations.

I recall the words of the great Parsi Prophet, Zoroaster: "Know well that a hundred temples of wood and stone have not the value of one understanding heart!" Understanding hearts are what we need, so that people may live and work in harmonious, peaceful co-existence!

Ego at the Workplace

Most of us spend well over two-thirds of our waking hours at the workplace. Today the working environment has become a tough, stress-filled competitive arena. There is a lot of talk about teamwork, but in reality, the team spirit is lacking. When there is lack of harmony between colleagues and a strained relationship with the superior officer, the workplace becomes a battleground!

Not only does this lead to what we call 'Monday morning blues' or a reluctance to return to work after the weekend; it is also bad for business; bad for the organization. When colleagues and superiors start to play the game of one-upmanship, productivity and organizational goals take a beating.

When egos are kept in check, we can focus on the task at hand and concentrate on goals that matter. We can approach people for help without feeling insecure; we can offer help without being afraid that we will be exploited.

Some years ago, I met a successful businessman who told me that the secret of his success was that he had gone ahead and hired employees who were smarter and more intelligent than him; he actually made this remark in the presence of his subordinate employees, whom he was introducing to me. This attitude reveals his trust and the level of confidence he has in his people.

Of course, disagreements are bound to happen at the workplace. It is not always possible for us to be 'nice' in a superficial way; brainstorming is done; options are thrashed out; pros and cons are discussed; in such a situation, feelings are not always considered; or at best, they are considered irrelevant.

But I feel it is possible to disagree politely. You can reject another's viewpoint without being rude or aggressive. You can take into account all suggestions and strive for a consensus. You can look at the issues dispassionately without letting personality clashes impede the outcome. Experts call this being solution-oriented rather than problem-focused.

"Let's focus on the product and not the people," a business leader is quoted as saying. I would not agree with that view. People are the ones who make or mar, sell or pull down products. When you have built up a team based on mutual respect, trust, friendship and a sense of belonging, you can give and take criticism in the right spirit.

I have come across many young people who have told me personal stories of being insulted, humiliated, demeaned and even yelled at by their superiors in the workplace. I cannot help feeling sad when I hear this. I believe it is possible for all of us to be firm and strict and impose discipline –

without being rude and angry and using harsh words or shouting at the top of our voice! What can we hope to gain by demoralizing the people who work for us?

Have you heard about the fond mother who said to the Nursery Class teacher, "If my Pinky misbehaves, don't yell at her; please scold the girl sitting next to her; Pinky is very intelligent and she will understand what is expected of her." The opposite is true of the workplace; if the girl sitting next to her is yelled at, Pinky may become demoralized and even disgusted! Shouting matches belong in the gladiators' arena; they vitiate the atmosphere of an organization. Ego clashes and bullying tactics can demoralize people who are not actually personally involved in the conflict.

Ego driven people can be destructive influences in the workplace. Their presence, their actions, their words and their attitude poison the work environment for everyone. When employees feel unappreciated and undervalued, they cannot give their best. While it is healthy to have differences of opinion, it is most unhealthy to have slanging matches and ego clashes.

A Management expert was asked, "What is the reason for ego clashes at the workplace?" His answer was disturbing. "Fundamentally, we are a species of animal, and we will indulge in conflict."

It is for us to decide whether we must stay at that level or evolve towards higher forms of existence.

And finally, a word for ego-driven superiors: you don't always have to be right. You must not take offence for the least reason. You may make mistakes and it is perfectly alright to admit the same. You don't have to undermine or insult others to prove your superiority. If you attempt to control others beyond a point, you will only exhaust them and drive them away.

Being polite, listening to your people is not a sign of weakness; but shouting others down definitely is! Bullying or bulldozing your employees is not a sign of strength; but encouraging them to have a sense of belonging and allowing them to be happy people is!

Set aside your Ego to Cultivate Better Relationships!

A well-known relationship expert remarks that the ego has no relationship skills! The ego tries to manipulate people by adopting various negative techniques like aggression, resistance, withdrawal and intolerance. Our hearts, on the other hand, rely on intuitive techniques like understanding, forgiveness, patience and trust, to nourish our relationships and take them forward. When our understanding hearts win the battle over the ego, relationships flourish; when ego takes over, relationships lose out.

How does ego manifest itself in ruining relationships? The signs are there for us to see:

1. We expect too much from others, and are not prepared to give as much as we take.

2. We cultivate a sense of entitlement; we imagine that the others are there to do what we need and make life easy for us.

3. We lap up praise and appreciation, but we are not prepared to appreciate others.

4. We become critical, even judgmental to the point of severity and harshness. We set impossibly high standards for others, which do not apply to us.

5. We cease to cultivate that wonderful 'attitude of gratitude' that makes lives meaningful.

6. We forget what it is to forgive with an understanding heart.

7. We live under the illusion that we don't have to apologise under any circumstances.

There are other extremes to which low self-esteem or a negative ego can take us: we may become passive or withdraw altogether; we can become depressed and frustrated; worst of all, we can try to erase our true nature in trying hard to be the kind of person that we imagine the other people expect of us. All this is not selfless; it is self-destructive.

How can we stop our ego from 'messing around' with relationships that matter to us? We cannot have 'theories' for everything –

especially for getting along with people. No blueprint can give us a preplanned design to organize our lives with other people. Human beings are unique, perhaps somewhat illogical, and definitely unprogrammable!

Each one of us is sensitive; each one of us is different; and each one of us is constantly variable—our mood and temperament change from day to day, may be even from hour to hour!

Every relationship is unique and special. Parents, spouses, children, family, friends, neighbours, colleagues, superiors, subordinates, employers or employees – every relationship needs to be nurtured with understanding and patience.

The secret of successful relationships is to be found in an understanding heart – preferably, your own!

Curbing the destructive ego in relationships

1. Always look for the merits in others: do not focus on their demerits. The secret of a harmonious and peaceful life is: Focus on people's merits and strengths – not on their weaknesses and defects.

2. Develop a healthy sense of humour, especially the wonderful ability to laugh at yourself. Learn to laugh with others; try a smile or a kind word – you will find that wrongs are easy to set right, and 'wrong doers' are set back on the right track!

3. Life is too short to be small. Let us not be small-minded. Let us be generous with praise, appreciation and encouragement.

4. When I find fault with others, I regard myself as superior – better than the others. This is pride, this is egoism. This must be overcome if we are to be truly happy.

5. Take the lead in appreciating others! Do not be calculative in giving and receiving praise. Human relationships thrive on caring, sharing and mutual appreciation. We rely on our loved ones, our friends and those closest to us, for moral support and encouragement. In this, as in other things, what we send out

comes back to us. For life is like a boomerang: what we are, what we do, comes back to us. When we give our best to the world, when we send out warmth, love and appreciation – it all comes back to us.

6. We often think of our friends, spouses and parents as 'pillars of strength' which are always there for our solid support. I urge you to occasionally think of them as precious plants that need constant tending!

When tensions are rising and troubles are mounting, it is people who are close to us that bear the brunt of our stress. We are often courteous, polite and kind to perfect strangers, but rude and brusque to our own spouses and parents.

Give your best to your loved ones and those closest to you. We often put on our best behavior and attitude to impress strangers. We reserve our nasty side for the benefit of those who are close to us.

7. Give time and effort to improve your relationships. Do not take people for granted. Many relationships suffer from sheer neglect and indifference. It was a wise man – perhaps, it was a wise woman – who said, "Even love has a shelf life."

8. Learn to listen to the people in your life. God gave us two ears but only one tongue in a single mouth. The moral of the story is that we must learn to listen more and talk less.

9. Value the people around you. Give people what they need – and a little more! Let us treat people as we would like to be treated by them. Who are we to judge another's worth? What if God were to apply the same scales to us as we apply to others? In this aspect, let us err on the side of generosity, compassion and kindness, so that God may look at us with mercy rather than justice.

10. Accept people as they are; do not try to mould them to suit your temperament and your requirements. Respect the individuality and the identity of others.

No man is an island,
No man stands alone,
Each man's joy is joy to me,
Each man's grief is my own.
We need one another,
So I will defend,
Each man as my brother,
Each man as my friend.

- Song by Joan Baez

(Based on an idea from John Donne's sermons)

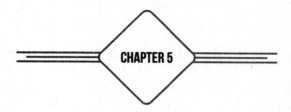

CHAPTER 5

OF WHAT ARE WE PROUD?

As long as you are proud you cannot know God. A proud man is always looking down on things and people: and, of course, as long as you are looking down you cannot see something that is above you.

- C. S. Lewis

Pride Personified

There is a wonderful short story by Rebecca Livermore that teaches us that if only we knew the truth about ourselves, we would never, ever be proud.

Long, long ago, in the Land of Judgement, there lived a girl. Her name was Pride. Pride was a very ordinary looking girl except for one peculiar feature: a twenty-foot-long wooden beam which protruded from her right eye. However, she could never see herself clearly even when she stood before the mirror, for the beam obstructed her vision. Thus her idea of what she looked like was very distorted. In fact, she couldn't even see the beam in her own eye.

"I think I'll go into the town square today she mused one day. I can't wait for everyone to see this new dress I picked up; it's finer than any other I have."

She smiled as she carefully dressed herself, taking great delight in putting on such costly attire.

As she hurriedly ate her breakfast, she thought contemptuously of all the people who lived in Judgement.

"I'm sure glad I'm not like Envy!" she thought. "She's such a loser. She goes around town wishing she was like everyone else. I'm glad I don't have that problem." Pride chuckled as she thought of the effect her new dress would have on Envy.

"And then there's Meekness. Talk about a wimp. She's about as bad as they come. If she wasn't so hopeless, I'd take her under my wing and teach her how to be more like me. But," sighed Pride, "there's no chance of that happening. Meekness could never be like me. Poor girl!"

"Look at everyone watching me" she thought with satisfaction, as she strolled through the town. "They must all notice I'm wearing a new dress." What she did not realise was that the people of Judgement were not looking at her new dress, but rather were gawking at the beam protruding from her eye. It seemed to be bigger every time they saw her.

She looked absolutely ridiculous! If it wasn't for the fact that she caused so much damage, the people of Judgement would probably find her to be rather amusing. But they had no time to laugh at Pride; they were too busy trying to get out of her way. If you got in her way, she could hurt you really badly!

"I wonder who will be knocked down first this time?" Gentleness asked. "I hope it's not Joy. She was so greatly injured the last time Pride came to town."

It didn't take them long to find out who would be hurt first. As soon as Pride turned to the right, both Mercy and Grace were knocked over by the beam in her eye. Pride just laughed as she saw them fall down before her. "What's wrong with these pathetic people anyway?" she questioned. "Every time I walk through town I see people falling down left and right."

Although the tool responsible for all the damage was right in front of her face, Pride was the only one in town who couldn't see it. She continued through town, causing havoc as she went.

Pride's thoughts were interrupted by a great commotion in the center of town. She didn't have to wonder what was happening for long, for when she looked up, she saw the Master Carpenter.

Pride didn't know too much about the Master Carpenter, but she knew she didn't like him. She shuddered as the Carpenter made his way toward her. Pride had never had a face-to-face encounter with the Master, and she wasn't looking forward to it. She tried to run away from him, but before she could, the Master Carpenter placed his hand on Pride's arm and said, "Your time has come."

The Master Carpenter began to quickly and skillfully hammer, file and saw away at the beam in Pride's eye. Piece by piece of the beam began to break. Pride began to feel lighter, and less weighted down, but the pain of the procedure was more than she was willing to bear. She tried to pull herself free from the grip of the Master Carpenter, and turned round when she caught a glimpse of herself in a mirror that hung outside the shop of her dressmaker.

Now that the beam was only a few feet long she was finally able to stand close enough to the mirror to be able to see it. She was taken aback to see how horribly ugly it was. She had seen specks of wood in other people's eyes, but never ever before had she seen such a horrendously large beam.

"How am I ever going to be able to remove this beam?" she wailed.

Then she heard a voice that was tender with compassion.

"Let me help you" the voice said.

As Pride turned toward the voice, she saw the Master Carpenter, standing there, with his hand extended toward her.

"Can you remove this beam?" Pride asked, sobbing.

"I can if you'll let me" responded the Carpenter.

"Will it hurt?"

"Beam removal is never painless. But besides being the Master Carpenter, I'm also the Great Physician. If you allow me to remove it, I'll anoint your eyes and bring healing."

Pride agreed to allow the Master Carpenter to do what was needed. Although it was painful, before she knew it, the beam was completely removed. As Pride held the beam in her hand, she was amazed by the ugliness and heaviness of it. She quickly laid it down at the feet of the Master Carpenter.

"Do what you will with it" Pride said.

In only a moment, the beam was gone. Then the Great Physician reached down and gently placed some ointment into Pride's eye.

He said, "Not only am I healing your sight, I am also giving you a new name. No longer will you be known as Pride. Your new name is Humility. Rest in my forgiveness and be healed."

He gently laid Humility down beside a quiet stream and caused her to fall into a deep, restorative sleep.

When Humility awoke, she felt lighter and more joyful than she ever had. As she sat up, she noticed an unusual box sitting at her feet. The box was oddly but beautifully constructed of bits and pieces of wood which were carefully sanded and perfectly joined together. Although she had never seen anything quite like it, the box looked strangely familiar.

All of a sudden, Humility realised that the Master Carpenter had crafted the box from the scraps of the beam which had been removed from her eye. She marveled at the work of art wrought from what had previously been so ugly.

After turning the box over and admiring it, she finally gained enough courage to open it. She was surprised to find the box filled with beautiful gifts: gifts of grace, mercy, joy, love, and forgiveness.

Humility stood up, and with the box in her hands made her way toward the town square. From the center of the town, she began to distribute the gifts the Master Carpenter had freely given her.

As she joyfully dispensed peace, love and joy to all who passed by, the Land of Judgement became the Land of Mercy, and joy, grace, love and forgiveness flowed freely through its streets.

Of what are we proud?

Many distinguished scientists have said that when man realises the vastness, the grandeur and the immensity of the universe we live in, and our own insignificance in the universal scheme of things, it is impossible for us to feel egotistical and proud. Just think – at one time, the universe existed; time existed; Creation existed; but planet earth did not exist; the solar system did not exist; man did not exist; and, in course of time, a day will come when this earth will cease to exist; and the solar system would have disintegrated. And yet, time will live on...

Of what are we proud, I often ask myself. Power, wealth, fame, youth, beauty - all, all are transient. As great ones have continually demonstrated even world conquerors leave this earth empty-handed. Sant Dadu Dayal tells us –

When one lost what was one's own, and abandoned all pride of birth: when vain-glory has dropped away, then, only then, is one face to face with the Creator.

It was the great Sufi saint Rumi, who said: "When thou thyself shall come to be, then the beloved Lord will thou find. Therefore, O wise man, try to lose thyself, and feel humility." He adds, for further emphasis, "Egoism and self-will are opposed to the Holy Name; the two cannot dwell in the same house. None can serve the Lord without humility; the self-willed mind is worthless."

Humility does not consist in hiding our talents and virtues, or in thinking of ourselves as being worse than we really are; but in realising that all that we are, and all that we have, are freely given to us by God. Therefore, as Thomas Kempis tells us, one of the best ways to acquire humility is to fix the following maxim in our mind: One is worth what he is worth in the eyes of God.

I remember vividly an incident which occurred when I was a child. I was doing my Geography homework one evening when a family friend walked into our house. His conversation was always loud. That day he began to boast about the row of buildings which he owned in Karachi.

"They occupy almost the whole street!" he asserted.

In my innocence and simplicity I went up to him with my atlas and said, "Uncle, will you be kind enough to point out your row of buildings on this map of India?"

Our friend was nonplussed. Karachi was indicated on the map by just a dot. How on earth could he mark out his row of buildings on that dot?

Guru Gobind Singh tells us:

Emperors before whom strong armed kings did meekly bow their heads in countless numbers:

Who possessed great elephants with golden trappings, proud and painted with brilliant colors:

Millions of horses swifter than the wind which bounded o'er the world:
What mattered it how mighty were these emperors?
All at the last went hence
With nothing, bare of foot.

Surely, our ancient rishis were right when they said: "I and mine are the greatest obstacles on the Godward path."

My Master, Sadhu Vaswani, described the way of love, the way of devotion, as 'the little way'. To tread the 'little way' he said, one had to be as humble as dust, realise one's nothingness, to 'lose' oneself, so that one could 'find' God. These are his beautiful words from the Nuri Granth, a compilation of his immortal songs of devotion:

What art thou?
A mere nothing!
Casting aside vestures of vanity,
Live as a lowly one!
In this speck of a universe,
Thou art but a tiny speck:
Why, then, art thou puffed up with pride?
Thou art but an insect:
Yet is thy head
Inflated with arrogance!

Ahamkara – the ego – is an abyss; it is the pit of pride, the pit of darkness, where dwells Satan, he taught us.

A very interesting story is related in the Mahabharata. The Kurukshetra war was over, and Sri Krishna had departed the earth. Arjuna was travelling across a strange country when he was attacked by robbers.

Now Arjuna was a fearless warrior, and had been the leading light of the Pandava forces in winning the war. Further, his weapons were all divine gifts. Therefore, he fought valiantly against his attackers – but it was to no avail. He was beaten and robbed.

Miserable and despondent, he sought out Sage Veda Vyasa and begged him to explain the inexplicable – how was it that he, the invincible Arjuna with his incomparable valour and weapons, faced defeat at the hands of a few ruffians?

Veda Vyasa explained to him that neither he, nor his weapons had possessed any intrinsic power. "Your invincibility came from the presence of the Lord who was your Divine Charioteer. It was His power too, that infused your weapons with their might. Now that He is no longer with you, these weapons are useless. And you fight now on your own feeble strength."

Arjuna's eyes were opened to a great truth. Man achieves all that he does only through the sanction and grace of the Divine Will!

We are only too apt to regard our cleverness, our skill, our diplomacy, our tact and our efficiency as the sole reason for our success. A little reflection will make us realise that it is the Divine presence that guides us at every step. Therefore, success and accomplishment should teach us humility instead of pride, and prompt us to express our gratitude to God.

Every accomplishment, every form of excellence, every success, small or big, belongs to God. If you are wise and intelligent, it is God-given. If your hard work and effort are commendable, it is due to the grace of God. If you are truly conscious of this, and acknowledge His grace in all humility – why, this humility too is a manifestation of His mercy upon you!

May I share a personal reminiscence with you? When I took leave of my near and dear ones and sought refuge at Gurudev Sadhu Vaswani's feet, the very first lesson he taught me was the lesson of humility.

"The God that rules millions is the ego," he said. "Enthrone God on your heart – the God of love – if you wish to cease wandering!"

When I asked him how I could enthrone on my heart the God of love, his answer was simple: "Be humble as ashes and dust!"

My Master said to me that his lonely heart was not in search of the proud of purse, the proud of power or learning, for the world was full of such people. He sought the company of the humble ones, the simple ones, of those who had reduced themselves to nothing, who had emptied themselves of all 'self' – so that they could be used by the Lord to do with them whatever He would.

"We are proud of our power and inventions," Gurudev Sadhu Vaswani said. "And yet, what are we? Grass that floats on a stream!"

"What is the mark of him who has attained?" I asked him one day. In his hand was a pencil. With it he drew the figure of a zero – 0 – and he said, "This is the mark of him who has attained: he becomes a zero."

And, on a green card, he wrote a brief message for those who had gathered for his *darshan* that day. The words were so penetrating that they have stayed in my heart, to this day:

Blessed be thou, if thou bend until thou break, becoming nothing, a zero! In the yoga (union) of two zeros is the One Infinite!

The truly humble are the truly happy. And what we need to be truly happy, is not a change in outer circumstances, but deliverance from slavery to the self, the petty ego. This petty ego sits as a tyrant on some of us, robbing us of the bliss i.e. our heritage as children of God. For God built this world in beauty, and we were meant to live our lives in the fullness of freedom and joy. Man was meant to live like a song-bird, unfettered, free. Alas, man finds himself cribbed, cabined, confined. He has become like a bird in a cage – he is trapped in the cage of self-centeredness!

Not until self-centeredness goes may man become truly happy and free: and the prison of self-centeredness opens with the key of humility. Especially important for the seeker on the path is humility: for it sets free the swan bird of the soul, and the soul can soar into radiance and joy!

⟡━◄◆►━⟡

Remembering that I'll be dead soon is the most important tool I've ever encountered to help me make the big choices in life. Because almost everything - all external expectations, all pride, all fear of embarrassment or failure - these things just fall away in the face of death, leaving only what is truly important.

- Steve Jobs

⟡━◄◆►━⟡

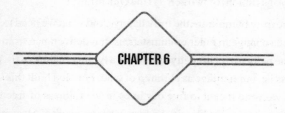

CHAPTER 6

BEWARE THE 'PRIDE' OF HUMILITY

Once the question of glory is settled, everything is settled. Resolve to give God the glory, and you'll know the answer to the vast majority of the decisions in your life.

If you're fighting with your spouse, what should you do? Whatever brings God the most glory. If you're disobeying your parents, what should you do? Whatever brings God the most glory. If you're disagreeing with leadership, how should you conduct yourself? In a manner that brings God the most glory. If you have aspirations, what should you pursue? Whatever brings God the most glory.

What you do, why you do it, how you do it, when you do it—humility considers every decision by asking, "Who gets the glory?"

- Pastor Mark Driscoll

Badge of Pride

There was once a church that realised the importance of humility, so it formed a committee to find the most humble person in the church. Many names were submitted and numerous candidates evaluated. Finally, the committee came to a unanimous decision. They selected a quiet little man who always stayed in the background and had never taken credit for his years of devoted service. They awarded him the "Most Humble" badge for his faithful service. However, the next day they had to take the badge away from him because he had pinned it on and was wearing it with pride!

Pride of Humility?

Is that a paradox or a contradiction in terms?

Alas, it is neither, I'm afraid, but the real state of affairs amongst many of us.

Whenever I talk about the pride of humility, I am reminded of how sorely Jesus was disappointed by some of the 'humble' religious teachers of his day. His disappointment is recorded in the Gospel according to St. Matthew.

In those days, the teachers of the Hebrew Law and the Pharisees (an exclusive set of religious preachers) had been given a really important task. It was their duty to teach and explain God's laws and commandments to the common people and also help the people to live by these laws. They were the interpreters and guardians of the Holy Laws whose sacred duty it was to teach, lead and guide the people in the ways of God. They were supposed to tell the people of God's love and mercy, His divine power and sanctity and to show them His love, His grace, His compassion and forgiveness. Alas, the reality was often very different!

Lord Jesus found that there were very many things that were wrong with them:

1. In the classic formulation of the Gospels, they did not practise what they preached. To quote the Prophet Isaiah, "These people come near to me with their mouth and honour me with their lips, but their hearts are far from me."

Faith, piety and true devotion are not just a matter of putting up a good show, a good 'performance'. We cannot put on masks of goodness or humility just to impress the world. We can't advertise selfless service and generosity and claim that we did it out of love and compassion. This is one of the reasons why cynics equate humility with hypocrisy.

2. These false teachers could not do what they expected the others to do. They encouraged people to obey God's laws, but they felt they were above such laws.

I am reminded of some of our politicians who deliver harangues against corruption and deceit!

3. These Pharisees loved to show off. We are told they wore little leather boxes tied against their foreheads – which ostensibly contained scriptural verses. The idea was to proclaim to the world that the holy texts were always carried on their person! "O, people, see how holy and devout we are!" they seemed to proclaim to the world.

One of our teachers had attended a Faculty refresher Course at the University some time ago. Ideally, these should be programmes where teachers are able to update their knowledge and get familiar with the latest trends and developments in their areas of specialisation. Many senior teachers and experts were on hand to share their knowledge and erudition with the teachers. But there was one young man, who arrived at the lectern carrying a dozen heavy volumes of encyclopedic and carefully, elaborately took his time, arranging them on the table. Some of the audience was mightily impressed by this impressive arrival. But alas, when his talk began, the teachers were only left bitterly disappointed. The young man had nothing worthwhile to share with them!

4. These people were proud of their grand titles and positions and loved to be bowed to and greeted in the synagogues and temples. They would of course bow low in acceptance of the reverence shown to them; but this was nothing but 'sanctimonious pride' to borrow yet another term from the scriptures!

Even today, we have people who insist on being addressed as Your Excellency, Your Honour, Esteemed, etc., etc. If you refer to a senior academician as Dr. so-and-so, he will sternly reprimand you and say, "I am a Professor." To a Pharisee who insisted on being called a teacher, Jesus said:

"You must not be called 'Teacher', because you are all members of one family and have only one Teacher. And you must not call anyone here on earth 'Father', because you have only the one Father in heaven. Nor should you be called 'Leader', because your one and only leader is the Messiah. The greatest one among you must be your servant. Whoever makes himself great will be humbled, and whoever humbles himself will be made great. (Matthew 23:8-12)

I wonder what our leaders and VVIPs will have to say to that!

5. As religious teachers, they insisted on putting themselves first. They sought their 'greatness' through their high handed ways and the pride of being 'leaders'.

"Seek not power, seek service!" was Gurudev Sadhu Vaswani's clarion call to us. "He is great who greatly serves." It is only vain people who mpride themselves on their titles and honours. Quantifiable assets, movable and immovable properties are of no concern in the Lord's eyes. It is the servants of humanity that receive His grace.

Jesus Christ himself was the very opposite of all these people! He preached nothing that he did not practice himself. He did not ask us to do anything that he himself did not do. He loved the people and he proved it through his thoughts, words and deeds. He allowed himself to suffer, he martyred himself on the Cross so that people might be redeemed through him.

Jesus was not only a picture of true humility, he placed humility above nearly every other virtue. "He that exalteth himself shall be abased, and he that humbleth himself shall be exalted;" "Blessed are the poor in spirit;" and in numerous other passages, we are reminded that God loveth the humble, but that he "bringeth down the mighty from their seats, and exalteth the humble and meek."

This is true humility that we refer to, not false modesty and hypocrisy.

A great nineteenth century Pastor tells us that pride is groundless; it is also brainless; it is self-consuming, for it feeds upon itself; it is ever changing, for you never know when it will rear its ugly head and in what context; people may be proud of their wealth, their power, their appearance, their qualifications or even their offspring. Pride, when it is most successful, stands in a slippery place. You can never say when it will come tumbling down!

When pride wears the garb of humility, it naturally assumes worse aspects, as it is masked by hypocrisy and false show.

Humility, as I said is not to be equated with false modesty. Humility is the intelligent and right estimate of oneself and one's abilities. To cloak oneself in false modesty, to hide one's true talents from the world is not humility. It is not humility to underrate oneself unnecessarily. Humility is to think of yourself as God would think of you! It is to acknowledge God's countless gifts to us with gratitude and to use those gifts in His service and in the service of His suffering children. Humility is to realise that all that we are, all that we have, is God's gift to us.

Above all, we would do well to remember, that humility does not dwell in the face; it dwells in the heart. It is not in sanctimonious looks, in bowing and scraping, in false modesty that we can see humility. This may deceive some people some of the time, but people will soon come to know that it is not the genuine thing!

The Humble Seeker

Many years ago, my Beloved Gurudeva told us the story of a seeker of God. In quest of the heaven-world, he moves, from place to place, and, after much weary wandering, finds himself standing at the gate of the heaven-world.

The gate-keeper asks him, "Who are you?"

And the seeker answers, "I am a scholar and a teacher."

"Wait here a while," says the gate-keeper, "I shall go in and report your arrival."

Soon, the gate-keeper returns with the answer, "I cannot let you in, for the Master says there is no place for teachers in the heaven-world."

I hope my teacher-friends are not upset by the course this story is taking: This story is about a teacher who had not yet found his true vocation. As Gurudev Sadhu Vaswani used to tell us, "So many teachers, are vain. They parade their little learning. How can there be a place in the heaven-world for those who live in a world of vanity?" But let us return to the story.

Disappointed, the seeker is about to turn away, when he hears the words, "O teacher! The dust of dead words clings to thee! Wash thyself of this dust in the waters of silence!"

The teacher follows the advice given to him. Every day he sits in silence and listens to the words of the saints and sages. Gradually, his 'self'–consciousness drops; he becomes humble. And one day, as he sits in meditation with a true longing in his heart for the Lotus-feet of the Lord, he hears the words:

"Blessed is the life of a helper and a servant! If you would enter the heaven-world, breathe out this aspiration that you may be a servant of all, a servant of teachers and pupils, of the lonely and lowly ones, of all men and birds and animals, a servant of God and His creation!"

The seeker breathes out this aspiration, again and again. And, all of a sudden, he finds himself back at the portals of heaven. This time, the gates of heaven are wide open. The angels are there to greet him, saying, "Blessed indeed are you, O servant of God and His suffering creation! Enter in and behold the Master's face – pure and fair, beyond compare!"

Yes, the Kingdom of God, the ashram of the Guru, the path of discipleship is only for the humble at heart. Unfortunately, many of us are proud, vain and lost in ego! When we are lost in ego, we become blind to wisdom, and can only wander from darkness to darkness!

───────────────◆◆◆───────────────

True humility has to do with acknowledging and respecting who you are and what you can do, without any outside confirmation or approval. False humility has to do with claiming you are less than you believe you are, and that you can do less than you believe you can. This kind of humility almost always requires outside confirmation or approval to cover up an inner feeling of arrogance. The person with false humility has a driving need to convince others of how humble he or she is. Sometimes this is because a person believes that any form of pride is bad, and sometimes an essentially arrogant person is using false humility as a way of disarming or manipulating other people. A truly humble person has no need for others to know how humble he or she feels, nor any fear of others knowing. A truly humble person feels neither superior nor inferior to anyone else.

- Serge Kahili King

CHAPTER 7

THE WITNESS OF THE GREAT ONES

Humility is a Divine property and the perfection of the Christian life. It is
attained through obedience. He who is not obedient cannot gain humility.
There are very few in the world today who have obedience. Our humility is
in proportion to our obedience.

- Elder Thaddeus of Vitovnica

Sri Krishna Shows the Way

In the great epic of Mahabharata we are told that Sri Krishna went to Hastinapur as an Ambassador of Peace. His mission was to restore cordiality and peace between the Kauravas and Pandavas. King Duryodhana assumed that Sri Krishna would stay with him in the royal palace. But that was not to be.

Vidhura's wife, who was a devotee of Lord Krishna, prays sincerely to have Him as their guest, in their humble abode. She calls out to Him, "O Sri Krishna! You are coming to Hastinapur, we will surely get your *darshan,* but how I wish we may offer you our loving hospitality!"

Even while she is praying, she hears the voice of Sri Krishna. She goes out running to see Krishna at her doorstep, and welcomes Him whole heartedly. She does not have much by way of cooked food to offer him, so she picks up a few bananas from inside the house, and offers them to the Lord. In her excitement and devotion, we are told that she pealed the bananas but threw away the fruit and gave Him the banana skins to eat. Sri Krishna savoured the banana skins, for they were offered out of true devotion.

While this was happening, Vidhura arrives and is shocked to see Sri Krishna eating banana skins. He gets upset and says to his wife, "Do you realise what you are doing? You are feeding the Lord with banana skins instead of the fruit!" She is oblivious of everything. Thus reprimanded, she begs Sri Krishna's pardon, but He laughs it all away!

She goes inside to cook food, and serves it to the Lord. Sri Krishna relishes the food as if it were *chappanbhog* – i.e. a delicious banquet of fifty-six varieties of delicacies. When Vidhur eats the first morsel of food, he realises that his wife had forgotten to put salt in all of the dishes. He rebukes his wife, "What's wrong with you today? Why is it that you are serving Him, our Lord, saltless food and banana skins?" Hearing this, Sri Krishna tells him, "Please do not be harsh on your wife. She has offered me the most delicious food I have ever eaten. It is like the divine nectar of the gods, because it is cooked with pure love."

Speak Sweetly, Walk Humbly!

The mark of true devotion – *bhakti* – is utter humility. Whenever and wherever a *bhakta* calls out to the Lord from the depth of his heart, with an intense yearning, the Lord responds without delay. He appears before the devotee, fulfilling her/his wishes.

Let me quote to you those beautiful lines which I heard an angel whisper in my heart:

Mitha bolan, niv chalan
Hathu bhe kuchch de,
Rab tina de paas,
Vo jin kiyun dhondhe.

In translation, this beautiful verse means:

Speak gently,
Walk humbly,
Give something in charity.
Then you need not to the forest go,
For the Lord is with you already!

If you do these things dutifully, then there is no need for you to go to a forest and meditate. There is no need for you to go in quest of God. For God, the Source of all Joy and Happiness will come in quest of you – and meet you.

A veritable roadmap for the Life Beautiful is given us in those three injunctions: (1) Speak sweetly (2) Walk humbly and (3) Give something in charity with your own hands.

When I put this across to one of my friends, he said to me, a little apologetically, "With all due respect to you Dada, if we walk humbly and talk gently in that big bad world out there, people will walk all over us! I am afraid, that in today's harsh environment, humility and gentleness are apt to be taken as signs of weakness, rather than goodness!"

I said to him, "I beg to differ with that view. On the contrary, I feel very strongly that there is an indefinable sense of dignity about every truly humble person."

The great saint, Sri Ramkrishna Paramhansa, used to tell his disciples, to deliberate on the *mantra: Na Hum! Na Hum! Tu ho! Tu ho!* I am nothing – Thou art all! Thou art the creator of this Universe. Me? I am nothing. When you realise your insignificance, you will automatically become humble.

Guru Arjun Dev, in *Sri Sukhmani Sahib,* says, 'The true *Brahma gnani* is one who lives in humility.' A true *Brahma gnani* is pure as a lily and humble as ashes and dust. He immerses himself in austerity and lives a life of simplicity.

It is said of Leo Tolstoy, the great Russian writer, that when he realised the truth of his being, he renounced his vast material wealth, high social status and power. He went and lived among the poor peasants of Russia.

Think of Sri Krishna, the Lord of the universe. He humbled himself to become the charioteer of his dear, devoted disciple, Arjuna. Maha Vishnu became *Partha Sarathi* to demonstrate to us his *saushilya* – the quality of gentle, loving kindness that we must all emulate.

Mahatma Gandhi's poverty and austere life style is a legend of our times. Clad in his loincloth and *angavastra,* he conquered a million hearts, as well as the might of the British Empire.

If you wish to be great and noble like these illustrious personalities, then you should be humble. So humble, that people should ask you, "Who is your Guru?" Looking at your personality, people will be drawn to your Guru.

In India, we have the beautiful tradition of greeting everyone we meet with folded hands and the reverential greeting: *Namaste!* It is a beautiful gesture of respect for the other person, and a spontaneous act of humility that ennobles both he who salutes and he who receives the salutation. It is ridiculous to think that we 'lower' our dignity in any way by saluting another thus: we would do well to remember that it is the God within the human form that we salute thus.

Why should we be humble in our dealings with others? Because Lord Krishna resides within every one of us. He is omnipotent, omnipresent, omniscient. Lord Krishna's beauty, art, intellect, knowledge and ability are supreme. We are like a speck of dust, insignificant before His power and magnificence. And yet, He comes to live in the humble abode of our heart. Should this not teach us to be humble? If Lord Krishna Himself resides in the people we meet, how can we presume to be haughty and proud before Him? Should we not be soft, gentle, reverential and sweet to the Lord?

Another thing necessary for all of us is humility of the heart. Be humble; be humble as a blade of grass. Once Gurudev Sadhu Vaswani was asked: What kind of persons would you like to associate with? Rich and famous, intelligent and scholarly, elitist and sophisticated, or beautiful and charming? Gurudev Sadhu Vaswani with a magical smile replied, "My heart moves out to those who are humble. For the humble are pure at heart. They are the loved ones." Therefore let us learn to be humble and earn the grace of God.

We are told that Philip II (the father of Alexander the Great) employed two men whose sole responsibility was to address him twice each day. Their morning duty? To say: "Philip, remember that you are but a man."And in the evening? To ask: "Philip, have you remembered that you are but a man?"

Many great men of the modern world were men of simplicity and humility. Indeed their humility served to set them apart and added to their greatness.

Gandhiji too, surprised people by his simplicity and humility. One day, Richard Cregg, an American admirer of Gandhiji's, arrived at the Sabarmati *Ashram* to meet the Mahatma. He was told that Gandhiji was in the common dining hall.

Cregg wondered if Gandhiji was having a meal and whether he would disturb him by calling on him then. However, he found the Dining Hall and entered inside only to find the great-souled leader seated on the ground, peeling vegetables for the morning meal.

"Come in, come in," Gandhiji greeted the visitor cheerfully. "I'm sorry you find me occupied with my duty at the ashram, but I'm delighted to meet you! Welcome to Sabarmati Ashram!" The American was overwhelmed by Gandhiji's utter simplicity. In a trice, he was sitting next to

Gandhiji, helping him with the vegetables!

Of the great emperor Shah Jahan, we are told, that during a hot summer night, as he was resting in his private apartments, he was suddenly overcome by thirst. He clapped his hands, as was his wont, to call a servant to attend to him – but it so happened that none of the palace servants happened to be nearby.

The emperor arose from his royal couch and went to the pitcher of water which was always kept near his bed. The silver jug was absolutely empty!

By now, the emperor was parched with thirst. He went out into the enclosed courtyard which adjoined his private chamber, for he knew there was a well there, from which he could draw water. As he was unused to this task, he hurt himself badly on the crank of the pulley, when he tried to haul the container of water towards himself. The pain in his hand was quite sudden and severe, and he actually cried out in agony. At that moment, the thought flashed across his mind that here he was, an emperor – but he was so inept that he could not even draw water from the well to slake his own thirst! O Beloved Lord!" he exclaimed, "I thank you for this experience. How foolish and clumsy I am – and yet, in thy inscrutable grace, Thou hast made me an emperor!"

It was the great Sufi saint Rumi, who said: "When thou thyself shall come to be, then the beloved Lord will thou find. Therefore, O wise man, try to lose thyself, and feel humility." He adds, for further emphasis, "Egoism and self-will are opposed to the Holy Name; the two cannot dwell in the same house. None can serve the Lord without humility; the self-willed mind is worthless."

We read an amusing anecdote about St. Peter who once stood at the Pearly Gates of Heaven, reading the judgements that admitted the Blessed Souls to God's presence.

To a rich philanthropist who had spent much of his wealth on feeding the poor, he said, "I was hungry, and you gave me to eat. So enter the kingdom of the Lord."

To a man of service who had dug canals and wells, and installed hand-pumps in remote draught-prone villages, he said, "I was thirsty, and you gave me to drink. So come in."

In the line stood a poor clown who had worked in a circus and made people laugh. He trembled as he stepped before the gates of Heaven. With bowed head he waited for St. Peter's judgement. St. Peter smiled and said to him, "I was sad and depressed, and you made me laugh. Enter the kingdom of Heaven."

Grace and Courtesy

Graciousness and humility are instinctive to great people. In fact their personalities are only further enhanced – even adorned – by this special quality.

At a grand banquet where President and Mrs. Roosevelt were present, an old man approached Mrs. Roosevelt and greeted her respectfully. She returned the greeting graciously and spoke to him for some time.

Emboldened by her courteous behaviour, the old man said to her, "Madame, may I bring my wife to you – she thinks the world of you – and she will be delighted to have the opportunity to meet you in person!"

"May I ask you how old your wife is, Sir?"

"She is about eighty-two, ma'am," the old man replied. "She is seated just outside this hall, in the anteroom. Shall I bring her here to meet you?"

"No, Sir," smiled Mrs. Roosevelt. "I should go and see her. You see, I'm fifteen years younger than your wife, and I should go to see her – not the other way round!"

Truly, Mrs. Roosevelt was adorned by her humility!

When the distinguished scientist, Sir Isaac Newton lay on his deathbed, a friend said to him, "It must be a source of great pride and gratification to you to know that you have managed to penetrate to the depth of nature's wonderful laws!"

"Far from feeling proud," Newton said to him, "I feel like a little child who has found a few bright coloured shells and pebbles, while the vast ocean of truth stretches unknown and unexplored before me!"

All men of true learning are truly humble!

It was John Ruskin who said, "The first test of a truly great man is his humility."

The great Chinese philosopher, Confucius, also tells us that humility is the solid foundation of all virtues.

Our ancient Indian sages and poets also admired humility as the greatest virtue in man. To illustrate this they compared a great man with a bountiful tree laden with fruit, which bows down with its load of fresh fruits.

Rahiman was a famous Muslim poet who wrote lovely lyrics expressing *prem bhakti.* He also happened to be a very rich man who spent his great wealth not on his own personal luxuries, but for the benefit of the poor and needy.

While he gave away alms to *sadhus* and *fakirs,* he always bowed his head low, and refused to look at them.

Noticing this, a friend asked him, "Why do you bow down your head while giving alms to the poor?"

"They praise me for my humble mite… which in reality is that of the Almighty," replied Rahiman. "I am only His agent, the instrument of His divine plan. Therefore I bow down my head in embarrassment, for I do not deserve their praise and thanks!"

The friend became speechless with admiration for Rahiman's humility.

Seek The Lowest Place

Thou shalt seek the lowest place! I wonder how many of you will abide by this commandment in this day and age when there is a scramble for power and greatness. Everyone is seeking the highest place! Governments are toppled; board rooms have become battlegrounds; sons oust their fathers; coups are staged; fierce rivalry and competition prevail. Everyone wants greatness!

But the true student of the Gita, the devotee of the Gita, will always seek the lowest place. This has been the witness of the great ones of humanity – and Sri Krishna himself demonstrates this wonderful ideal to us, by his own personal example. He lived as an equal, albeit a much loved, much spoilt son of Gokul. He played with the *gwalas,* stole butter from the kitchens of the *gopis,* made mischief with the boys and played games with the girls in Brindavan. He never, ever forgot the humble friends of his youth and childhood; how delighted he was to receive his dear friend Kuchela, when the latter went to visit him in Dwaraka!

Think of how Sri Krishna comes on the battleground of Kurukshetra – not as a leader, not as a general, not as the king of Dwarka, but as *Parthasarathi – Partha's* (Arjuna's) charioteer. He comes as the driver – as we would call him today – of his dear, devoted disciple and friend, Arjuna.

Think of Jesus Christ. At the Last Supper, on the eve of his crucifixion, in the very last hours of his earth pilgrimage, he picks up a bowl of water and a towel, and he washes and wipes the feet of his own disciples. He also tells them words which we would do very well to heed: "He that would be the greatest among you, let him be a servant of all."

This is the witness of the great ones – they seek the lowest place.

He that is down need fear no fall
He that is low no pride:
He that is humble ever shall
Have God to be his guide.

These are the words of John Bunyan in his book, Pilgrim's Progress.

Think of Gurudev Sadhu Vaswani. One day some of us were sitting in a group, allotting duties for the *Janmashtami langar* which was to be held a few days later. Gurudev Sadhu Vaswani saw us and enquired as to what we were discussing.

"We are allotting duties to each one for the *langar,* Dada," we said to him.

"What duty are you giving me?" he demanded of us.

One of us said to him, "Dada, it will be wonderful if you could join us during the *langar*. Your 'duty' would be to remain seated at the entrance to the hall where *langar* is held – and to bless each one who enters to take his or her place in the hall. That would really make our day!"

"No," said the Master. "I will take a different duty. I shall sweep the floor after each batch has eaten, to get the hall clean and ready to receive the next batch." He always sought the lowest place!

The Gita tells us to walk the little way, to walk the way of humility. This is the way on which the grace of God will be poured upon us abundantly! God's grace is like holy water – and water, as you all know, seeks the lowest place. If you have occupied the lowest place, the grace of God will flood into your life, and you will not only be truly blessed, but you will also be a source of blessing to many!

Holy men and sages tell us that humility is the true mark of the evolving soul. You may be assured that it is not easy to attain – for it involves the utter effacement of the ego.

Humility Is Not Weakness

Someone asked Mahatma Gandhi, "Why are you called Mahatma, or great soul?" Gandhiji replied, "Because I consider myself the least of human beings." What he meant was that one had to take the lowest place possible, in order to become truly great in the eyes of God. Therefore Gandhiji always remained humble – always a student, always a servant of others.

Let me warn you too, against false humility or superficial humility. I am sorry to say that people often assume false humility for a particular purpose. Thus subordinates bow and scrape before their superiors. When you assume false humility for a selfish purpose, it is not really humility at all – but hypocrisy!

Even the greatest among us fall victims to the ego. The Mahabharata tells us the story of how the Pandavas were taught valuable lessons in humility, which made them better human beings.

Bhima learnt his lesson when Draupadi begged him to bring her a rare flower. She had been captivated by the fragrance of the flower, and wanted more like it. Eager to fulfill his beloved's every wish, Bhima set out to get the flower.

As he crossed the rocky paths and thick forests at breakneck speed, Bhima approached a grove, where a huge monkey lay across his path.

"Get out of my way," he snarled at the creature. "I'm in a hurry, so don't keep me waiting."

The monkey opened its eyes and looked at him sleepily. "I am too old and tired to move," it said to Bhima. "Why don't you just lift my tail and shift it to one side, so that you may pass me?"

Arrogantly, Bhima started to lift its tail with disdain, but to his utter shock and dismay, he could not even stir it! Gritting his teeth, summoning all his strength, he tried hard to push the tail away. He was now perspiring heavily, and his breath was gasping – but he could not budge the tail even an inch.

In an instant, Bhima realised that this was no ordinary old monkey, as he had assumed it to be. Filled with humility, he bowed down to the monkey and said, "Please reveal your true identity to me. I have learnt a valuable lesson from you today."

The 'old monkey' revealed himself to be none other than Hanuman, beloved of Sri Rama. He had come to meet Bhima, test his strength and bestow his blessings upon him. For both of them were sons of Vayu, the Wind-God. When Hanuman embraced him and blessed him, Bhima felt a fresh energy, a new spirit and immense strength flowing into his body – much stronger now than the inflated, egotistic personality which he had asserted a short while ago!

When the Kurukshetra war was over, Arjuna prepared to alight from his Chariot. He was proud of his might and valour, which had been the chief factor in defeating Kauravas. How many *astras,* how many celestial weapons had been directed against him! But he had bravely stood his ground against them. They could not even touch him! Now it was time to leave the battleground, and rest his weary limbs.

Before he alighted, Arjuna said to Sri Krishna, "Please alight now, Lord. You must be tired too!"

"After you, Arjuna," said Sri Krishna with a smile. "I am your *Sarathi*. How can the driver alight before his passenger does? You must be the first to get off."

Delighted by the Lord's gracious reply, Arjuna descended from the chariot and prepared to hold the reins of the horses, so that Sri Krishna could alight. But to his surprise, Sri Krishna asked him to go away, and stand at a distance.

When Arjuna was at a safe distance, Sri Krishna alighted from the chariot. In a moment, the chariot was blown to pieces, disintegrating before their very eyes!

Arjuna realised that what had kept him alive and prevented his chariot from utter destruction was not his valour, but the Lord's presence. It was Sri Krishna's grace and power that had stopped all the celestial weapons hurled at Arjuna. If the Lord had alighted from the chariot first, Arjuna would have been blown to bits without His divine protection. This was why Sri Krishna had asked him to walk away before He Himself alighted from the chariot, thus making it defenceless and subject to the power of the various *astras* (weapons) hurled against it!

Humility is not weakness: I regard it as a truly powerful weapon that can break the tyranny of the ego!

―――――――――――◦◦◦◦◦―◦◇◦―◦◆◦―◦◇◦―◦◦◦◦◦――――――――――

An inflated consciousness is always egocentric and conscious of nothing but its own existence. It is incapable of learning from the past, incapable of understanding contemporary events, and incapable of drawing right conclusions about the future. It is hypnotized by itself and therefore cannot be argued with. It inevitably dooms itself to calamities that must strike it dead.

- Carl Gustav Jung

―――――――――――◦◦◦◦◦―◦◇◦―◦◆◦―◦◇◦―◦◦◦◦◦――――――――――

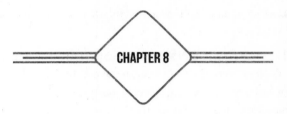

THE SLAYER OF THE EGO - WHY WE NEED THE GURU

Guru-Bhakti Yoga *is the surest and best* Sadhana *to destroy arrogance and to dissolve the vicious ego. Just as a particular deadly germ can be annihilated only by a certain specific chemical germicide, even so, to destroy* Avidya *and* Ahankara, *this unique* Guru Bhakti-Yoga *is the peerless specific. They are the gravest 'Mayacide' and 'egocide'. They become quite powerless and no longer afflict the fortunate soul who saturates himself with the spirit of* Guru-Bhakti-Yoga. *Blessed indeed is the man who earnestly takes to this* Yoga; *for he will obtain crowning success in all other* Yogas. *To him will accrue the choicest fruits of perfection in* Karma, Bhakti, Dhyana *and* gnana.

- Swami Sivananda

Where is your Ego?

An emperor once visited Bodhidharma with an urgent problem.

"There is a lot of restlessness inside me. I am very ambitious. Although I possess one of the greatest empires in the world, the ego still feels dissatisfied."

Bodhidharma smiled and said, "You have come to the right person. You only need to do one thing: come to me early in the morning, at four. And don't forget to bring your ego. If you don't bring it, there is nothing I can do."

The emperor felt a little confused and asked, "What do you mean?"

Bodhidharma said, "I mean exactly what I say. Bring your ego and I will put an end to it forever."

The emperor couldn't sleep that night. He tried to forget about it all and not to go, however he was also curious about this special man. He had met many wise men and great saints, but no one had ever said to him, "Bring your ego and I will put an end to it forever."

Finally he decided to go. And Bodhidharma was already waiting on the ground. Trembling, the emperor approached him. Bodhidharma said, "Alone? Where is your ego?"

The emperor replied hesitantly, "It is not something I can bring. It is always in me."

Bodhidharma said, "Then it is all right. Sit down, close your eyes and try to discover where exactly within you it is hiding. The moment you get hold of it, tell me."

Still trembling the emperor sat alone in the little temple outside the town and for the first time in his life he closed his eyes to meditate. He looked about within himself: where is the ego? An hour passed and another hour.

The sun rose and the emperor was in a state of bliss. Bodhidharma shook him up and said, "This is enough – two hours! Where is it?"

And the emperor started laughing. He bowed his head, touched Bodhidharma's feet and said, "I cannot find it."

Bodhidharma laughed and said, "See! I put an end to it. Whenever that strange idea about your ego comes up again, don't ask others how to relinquish it but close your eyes and try to find out where it is."

Discover the Light Within!

Aham Brahmasmi, our scriptures teach us. I am Brahman!

True, the light of the *Paramatman* shines within each one of us: but alas, we live in the outer darkness, unaware of the Light within. Like a prince who is mad about hunting, we are engaged in chasing material pleasures in the forests of the senses. What do we know of the indwelling Light?

Let me repeat, the Light inextinguishable dwells within each one of us, but we cannot see it, for it is hidden behind veils of ignorance, veils of mind and matter. The great wall of the ego stands between us and the *Paramatman* – and we cannot see the Light Divine. It is the Guru who can destroy the great wall of the ego, and lead us from darkness to light.

Why do we need the Guru? The Guru is the great cleanser, a great purifier – not merely a great teacher. Caught in the web of *maya,* caught in the snare of sensual desires and worldly pleasures, we accumulate bad *karma,* birth after birth after birth. Alas, our poor efforts are not enough to cleanse these impurities. But the Guru's grace can cleanse us and lead us towards the Divine Light of God.

The "Third Eye", the Inner Eye of the Spirit remains closed for most of us, its vision impaired by our bad *karma.* The cataract of the ego, the veils of arrogance and pride, have covered this inner eye completely. The Guru is the 'eye' surgeon, who can restore our inner vision.

The Guru reaches out to us, and with his grace, annihilates the ego; he tears away the veils of ignorance which shield us from self-realization; he reveals our true identity to us – *Tat Twam asi!* That art Thou! It is his grace that liberates us from bondage to the circle of life and death. This gift of Grace has devolved on the Guru from God Himself – for God knows that the world is in dire need of Grace. His Presence is of course Universal: He gives us the Guru, for our individual benefit, for our personal liberation. This is why, our ancient scriptures enjoin us to venerate the Guru as God:

> *Gurur Brahma, Gurur Vishnu*
> *Gurur Devo Maheshwara…*

The Guru is like Brahma; he creates us anew; he is like Vishnu, for he protects our immortal spirit, the *atman;* how is he like Maheshwara?

It is the constant endeavour of the Guru to destroy our "ego" which, in reality, has no existence, but is a mere shadow. The Guru draws us to himself through the irresistible power of his love – and then weans us from the "ego". He takes up the *trishul* (the trident) and strikes the 'ego'. In the process, the disciple may have to undergo great mental torture. Blessed is he who does not resist and says to the Guru, "My body and my mind, all that I have and I am, I offer unto thee! Do with me what thou wilt!"

Life is a process in which we try to detach the ego (the 'I') from the deeper consciousness of our self. The 'I' is attached to wealth, status, power, position, youth, possession, career and relationships. Being bound by so many attachments, it is constantly subject to fluctuation and change. We are sad, happy, elated, grieved, depressed, disappointed, thrilled, excited and swayed by one thing or another. As long as we are moved by these attachments, we are like the bound men in Plato's cave. When we resolve to break the bond and seek the Light, it is the spiritual teacher who can show us the way.

We must realise the truth once and for all – on our own, we are nothing; we can achieve nothing. The more we strive to be humble, the more subtle our ego becomes, so subtle that it is only the Guru who can detect it. This is why we need Him as our guide and guardian, at every step, in every stage of life. Other 'experts' are of no avail: only an evolved soul, as Friend of God, one who has seen God and known God, who lives and moves and has His being in God – only he can help us on the path of *shreya*. And so, Gurudev Sadhu Vaswani writes:

> Can you leap without feet?
> Can you smile without lips?
> Can you rest without sleep?
> Nor can you find the way – The True way – without the Guru.

Why do we stumble, when we set out on the path? The *vasanas* are subtle – the ego is subtle – and the Guru must eradicate them with His grace.

We are limited, finite beings, and with a load of *karma* that we carry, we are struggling up the narrow, steep path of *shreya*. The wise ones warn us that this path is so narrow, that two cannot walk abreast on it. We have to walk alone.

But there is an invisible hand that guides us; an effulgent light that shines before us. This is the light of the Guru's grace. He knows well, the twists and turns and curves on the path that we must not stumble upon. His light will enable us to see the truth, remove the obstacles from the path and help us proceed slowly but steadily towards the destination.

The light shines because of His grace; the hand guides us, because of His grace. We are on our feet and walking, only thanks to His grace.

There are times on the journey – and every aspirant knows this – when we are ready to give up, ready to turn back on the goal. We are discouraged, disillusioned. God does not seem to hear us or see us; we even begin to wonder if He is aware of our very existence and the struggle we are going through to attain Him! Of what use is this effort, we ask ourselves. It is taking us nowhere! Better to give up this phantom-chase and turn back to the material world, where our achievements are real and measurable!

And so we turn back on the path – if the Guru is not there with us. But if He is there, He will not let us give up the struggle. Whether or not we are capable, He is determined that we should succeed in our efforts!

"The Guru," Gurudev Sadhu Vaswani said to us, "is the lift to raise us to the heights, the lift which may take little ones (aspiring souls) to the Kingdom of God."

The Guru's Grace is Essential

Where would we be without the Guru's grace? The Tamil Saint, Manikka Vaasakar sings:

> To me, low as I was, Thou didst grant grace
> That I……. should melt in Divine love
> Thou cam'st in grace upon this earth
> To show Thy essential grace – more precious than a mother's love!

Man, today has become a traveler in space. He has set out on the outward journey: he has landed on the moon. He wishes to build colonies in space. But when he learns to look inward, when he sets out in quest of his true self, the *Atman,* he will *realise* his true nature, his innate Divinity. He will begin to live the true life – the life that is lived in God.

But there need not be a punishing effort; there need not be a severe struggle to undertake this journey. There is an effortless way. As the river flows on, singing its songs to the moving winds and the patient trees, as the river glides on without effort, even so can we live life in the effortless way – when we hand our lives over to the Guru.

The spirit of true surrender to the Guru is born out of humility, faith and devotion. It is born out of the annihilation of the ego. It is faith that gives the disciple absolute confidence in the Guru; it is faith which makes him repose all his trust in the Guru; it is faith that gives him the firm conviction that the Guru's words are the highest truth.

The disciple who is blessed with such faith does not argue; does not debate; does not analyse the pros and cons of surrender. He just surrenders himself at the Guru's feet.

Surrender is not servitude; surrender is not abject slavery. Surrender involves the highest *sadhana*. If there is anything we "give up" in surrender to the Guru, it is our lower nature, our 'almighty' ego, our selfish interests and desires, our negative ideas, prejudices, preconceived notions and biases. All of these constitute a terrible burden that we carry – and for which there is no place when we undertake our spiritual journey. They constitute an 'excess baggage' which we cannot carry on to a higher plane.

Therefore, to surrender to the Guru, is to assume command over your lower self. Do not make the mistake of imagining that it is slavish, it is beneath your dignity, and that you are giving up your freedom to another. If this is your notion, it were better far that you didn't seek a Guru, nor even think of taking the ultimate step of self-surrender.

If truth were to be told, many of us are abject slaves of our own desires, vanity and ego. If you wish to attain victory over the self, surrender to the Guru is a very necessary, preliminary step. But remember, he who conquers ego is a true hero. He is truly liberated and free. It is to achieve this victory, this freedom that a disciple surrenders to the will of the Guru. Now decide for yourself: will you be a slave to your lower self of desires and passions? Or would you rather be a devoted disciple of your *Guru*, and conquer your lower self, making your ego your slave?

As I have said to you again and again, the ego is like a cataract that blocks our inner vision. The Guru is the specialist who must perform a surgery to remove this cataract and restore our vision. When we take refuge in the Guru, this 'operation' becomes possible – and it is for our own good.

A more worthwhile question to ponder is – are we capable of such complete and spontaneous surrender, which involves the utter negation of the ego and self-will? The answer for many of us must be – NO.

Therefore, it is advisable that we undertake preliminary exercises which will deepen and strengthen our faith, and cultivate our devotion and self-control. One of the best ways to undertake this *sadhana* is meditation on the Guru, his beloved face, his lotus feet and his words of wisdom. When we hold his image in our hearts, offer our devotion to him and meditate on his words constantly, surrender becomes an achievable goal. The Guru's grace and power, charge and re-charge our innate spirituality; and this inflow of power weakens the ego and the *vasanas* which bind us.

Surrender To The Guru

I have spoken of 'unconditional surrender'. This is a *sadhana* that asks no questions, raises no doubts and seeks no 'reasons'.

Strange are the ways of the intellect. I have heard people arguing that *soham* (the *mahavakya* I am That) is for *advaitis* (non-dualists), while surrender is for *dvaitis* (dualists). This is a needless inquiry. To quote Sri Raman Maharishi, "In reality there is neither *dvaita* nor advaita, but that which is."

In South India, before a *havan* or *pooja* begins, they make a tiny little image of Ganesha with gur *(jiggery)* and dedicate the *pooja* to him. And, if no *prasad* or *naivedya* is available immediately, they 'pinch' a little gur from the Ganesha they made – and offer it to him as *naivedya*.

So it is with self-surrender to the Guru. We say, we offer body, soul, mind and possessions to God – but were they ours in the first place that we 'offer' them to Him who gave them to us?

When this false ego goes, this illusion of the 'I' disappears; it is much easier to practise surrender. And in the experience of many aspirants, it is easier to surrender before the visible, familiar, beloved form of the Guru, with whom we are able to establish the highest form of human relationship.

Some aspirants demand to know whether they can experience 'increased grace' and 'greater blessings' through surrender.

My answer to them is this: do not surrender with any expectation or desire. When you expect or desire something, you are still stuck with 'I' and 'Mine'.

Yet another query is: "Why is there no help or grace even after we surrender?"

If you have truly surrendered, how can you have complaints and grievances? When you surrender truly, you must be able to abide by the will of the Guru, and not insist on what pleases you.

Complete surrender is, perhaps, not possible for beginners. But the practise of even partial surrender will lead to peace and tranquility, and eventually, make complete surrender possible.

Shri Sai Baba of Shirdi tells us that firm and unfaltering faith in the Guru is the ultimate *sadhana*. "Trust in your Guru completely," he advises his devotees. "This is the only *sadhana* you need." The more one gives of oneself, the more one becomes capable of receiving the Guru's grace. Nor is there a sense of barter or give-and-take. The disciple voluntarily offers himself – and the Guru's grace is also spontaneous and unstinted.

Many of his devout disciples regarded Shirdi Sai Baba as the Guru incarnate. There was about him, a deep spiritual beauty and simplicity, which made them aspire to surrender to him utterly. And to them, he gave the promise of spiritual refuge. "Cast your cares upon me," he invited them. "Why should you fear, when I am near?" Who could resist such a compassionate offer of protection as this? It was to Sai Baba that people turned, rather than to an abstraction called God, whom they could not visualise. And Sai Baba made the Guru an indispensable facet on the *bhakti marga* or path of devotion. Apart from powerful revival of the *bhakti marga,* he was also responsible for resurrecting the traditional ideal of reverence for the spiritual Guru.

Down the ages, spiritual leaders like Sri Ramanuja and Samarth Ramdas and many others, have advised us to venerate those who can lead us to God, and to offer reverence and devotion to them as embodiments of the Divine. When we see him in this light, the Guru is God's medium, a receptacle of God's grace. Such a one can inspire and exalt us, and bring out the latent spiritual impulse in us. When we surrender to him, in truth, we surrender to God.

Some people point to the contradiction explicit in the goal of enlightenment -- freedom – and the way of surrender. Enlightenment, they argue is an all-knowing state, while surrender is relinquishing control over ourselves and our lives into others' hands.

Let me quote the words of an aspirant:

Our problem is that we don't want to surrender what we can surrender, and we do want to surrender what we can't surrender.

Surrender is not giving up your duties and responsibilities: surrender does not involve withdrawal to a forest of meditation and turning your back on your commitments and *karma yoga*. Surrender means giving up one's selfishness, one's individual desires, likes and dislikes for the sake of a higher goal – like self-realisation.

But you must remember one thing: the Guru does not force you to surrender to his grace. He wants nothing, desires nothing from you personally. He is beyond desire and expectation, utterly without selfish motives. Surrender – the impulse to surrender to one whom you regard as a worthy master – comes from within you.

The Guru does not enforce surrender upon you. In fact, you must remember that when you surrender, you surrender to your highest self. How can the Guru derive any benefit from your surrender? He knows only one thing – to give, give, give – to ever transmit the true knowledge and the light divine – and he goes on giving.

Are You Afraid of the Guru?

Sometimes, people have irrational fears about their Guru. Perhaps they perceive him through the veil of ignorance which causes misjudgement and misapprehension. They feel that they will lose their individualities and independence by surrendering to the Guru. They are afraid he "will take everything away and make them suffer".

This is misconception of the worst order!

To the beginner on the path, and even to aspirants who have been on the path of *sadhana* for some time, the pull of *maya* and the lower self is very strong indeed! Perhaps for some of us, it is stronger than even the Guru's *shakti* to uplift us. This only means that we must acquire inner strength by overcoming these negative powers.

No one can give you a theory of self-surrender, or teach you how to go about it! It comes from within: it is born out of deep love, devotion and faith to God and Guru.

Let me repeat: the Guru asks for nothing; the Guru wants nothing from you. In ancient India, the Guru's lived in *ashramas* or forest hermitages, where disciples came to live with them, serve them, and imbibe knowledge at their feet. But this life of simplicity and service was for the disciple's own benefit and inner growth. This is why our ancient scriptures tell us to give whatever we have to the Guru: but the Guru is enjoined to accept nothing but the disciple's ignorance.

It is the true Guru who can destroy your false ego and lead you on to the God within you.

The Guru spells death to the ego. The Guru does not have to implant God within you, because He already exists there. All that the Guru does is clean away the accumulated dirt and dross that has soiled the mirror of your heart – and when the ugly stains of the ego are removed, you behold the Beloved reflected therein.

There are many 'professional' seekers among us today. They go forth from one Guru to another, rejecting each for one reason or another. They are haunted by their own ego, their pride of knowledge and arrogance over their *sadhana*. They imagine they are perfectly apt in meditation and renunciation, and need the Guru only for namesake. The Guru must perforce perform 'surgery' on their ego, before they can receive anything from him!

"I know this," "I can do this," "I am such a one," "I am the doer," "I am the giver," – how vain and futile are such assertions!

Here is how a great poet saint puts it:

When my ego was struck by the sword that is the Guru's love,
That love began to kill my ego.
Even when I was alive, I experienced death.
My death died; and I became immortal.

The ego is subtle; its workings are not obvious. As the seeker is making progress on the path, he may pride himself on his efforts. Sometimes he thinks he is close to success. Sometimes he feels he has attained his goal. Sometimes he realises with despair, that it is very difficult to be spiritual.

Then comes to him the realisation that his efforts and endeavours are not pure but tainted, spotted. The darkest spot of them all, he realises, is the ego – the lower self – the 'I'. And then he begins to realise that he must transcend the ego to enter into the Limitless. He begins to realise that of his own accord, he can do nothing, achieve nothing. He learns to accept all that comes to him – abasement, criticism, disappointments – as the Will of God. As the love of God and Guru fills him, egoism dies.

A Pandit, well-versed in the *shastras,* once came to meet Gurudev Sadhu Vaswani. "Is it not true that a deep study of the *shastras* can help the seeker on the path?" he asked the Master.

Gurudev Sadhu Vaswani answered, "The *shastras* are often studied as an intellectual exercise, and often their students quarrel among themselves over the interpretation of the texts. The darkness of a room is not dispelled by uttering the word "Lamp"! So too, the darkness of the ego cannot be removed by the word-meaning of the spiritual texts. This darkness will not be dispelled until the 'inner light' is unveiled. And the inner light is unveiled through that illumined one whom we call the Guru."

We read many books – but to the pilgrim on the path, books may be a burden. We study the lives of saints – but of what avail is this study if our daily lives do not bear witness to it? Every morning, we read from the scriptures – but are we any better than parrots who recite again and again, the name of God? We go to the *satsang* every evening without fail – but are we better than a temple bell which, at the exact hour, calls the *devotes* for worship?

The one great barrier between us and Self-realisation is the ego. Alas, instead of putting it down, we strengthen it; we hug it to ourselves as if it were our dearest friend. Our actions, our thoughts, our flights of imagination only feed the ego – until the ego becomes our master and lord.

Let us break the tyranny of the ego!

I think once you have set your foot on the spiritual path, all you are required to do is to beware of the ego.

The spiritual path is the path of annihilation of the ego. It is not what you do that matters, it is the way you do it. If your actions inflate your ego, refrain from doing them. If it deflates your ego, you are on the right path.

Never do a thing which inflates your ego. If there is one thing that stands between you and your Guru, if there is one thing that stands between us and God, it is the ego.

It is like this. The sun is shining. Suppose we cover our eyes with the palm of our hand the sun will not be seen by us. The sun is 91 times bigger than the earth, but it can be hidden with the palm of our hand. Similarly, the ego is very small. But because we magnify it in our daily life beyond all proportion, it has come and taken hold of us.

Guru-*bhakti yoga* is something that all of us can practise in this *Kaliyuga* – and it is the shortest, easiest and quickest way to reach God. The practice of this *yoga* breaks the fetters of egoism and enables us to cross the dreadful ocean of *sansarsagar*. And obedience to the will of the Guru is a great virtue – for it negates self-will, egoism and indiscipline, and inculcates the divine qualities of humility, self-surrender and devotion.

Will the sage close to the Tao become extinct
in a world where the ego is the norm?
Will despair drive the sage from the Tao
as his compassion turns to bitterness?
Isn't it inevitable
in a world ruled by ignorance
that the new-born mind becomes a stranger to itself
even before it can take its first tentative steps?
Isn't innocence being destroyed by greed
even before the innocent have a chance to make a choice?
Isn't our harmony with the Tao irretrievably lost?

Do not despair.

The Tao is in us;
and we are in the Tao.
There is no separation
from the Tao.

Like a flash of lightning
illuminating the night sky,
one instant of enlightenment
once in a thousand years
will drive ignorance away.

(The Tao is Tao, 49)

SECTION II
BREAK THE TYRANNY OF THE EGO!

PRACTICAL SUGGESTIONS

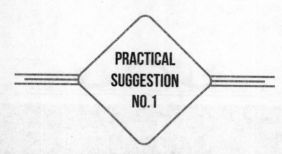

PRACTICAL
SUGGESTION
NO. 1

WHEN IN THE MIDST OF FRIENDS OR STRANGERS, DO NOT TRY TO SHOW OFF

Perhaps the less we have, the more we are required to brag.

- John Steinbeck

The Boasting Traveler

A man who had traveled widely in foreign lands had such a swollen head when he returned to his homeland, that he just could not stop boasting about his travels and all the countries he had visited and the wonderful things he had seen and done there. Needless to say, he was the hero in each and every one of his boastful accounts.

Rhodes was one of those cities he had happened to visit. Among other things, he said that when he was at Rhodes he had leaped to such a distance that no man of his day could leap anywhere near him. In fact, he boasted, there were very many great athletes in Rhodes at the time he was there, but not one of them could match his feat. He could call any one of them as witness, he claimed, to prove how high he had leaped.

One of the bystanders interrupted him, saying: "Now, my good man, if all this is true, where is the need for a witness? Just suppose this to be Rhodes and leap for us."

This famous fable by Aesop gave rise to the ancient Roman satiric saying: "Hic Rhodus, hic salta!" — "Rhodes is here, here perform your jump."

Boasting Puts People Off!

What is boasting? It is talking with excessive pride about oneself; it is showing excessive self-satisfaction about one's achievements. The ancient Greeks referred to it as *hubris*. i.e. extreme pride and overconfidence, leading to a loss of touch with reality. In ancient Greek theology and philosophy, *hubris* was a spiritual as well as psychological lapse. It is an accepted fact in Greek thought that *hubris* would always be followed by punishment. Thus we have the saying: "Pride goes before a fall".

In more down-to-earth terms, we refer to chronic boasting as self-promotion today.

Why does boasting put most people off?

It is not that people do not like to listen to other people's success stories. On the contrary, a success story, especially of the rags-to-riches or the life-transforming variety always inspires and motivates us. What makes boasting so unacceptable is that the person who boasts is not in the least interested in inspiring or motivating others; in fact, he is not even interested in others. Boasting becomes a one way street through which they want to toot their horns (in some cases blare out their horns) to make all the world around them aware of their feats.

Psychologists tell us that boasting does good for our morale and self-confidence; but they add a proviso, a very important one: boast to yourself, about yourself! That is, give yourself a private pep-talk. Tell yourself that you have done very well, and that you congratulate yourself on your achievements, big or small. In other words, give yourself a pat on the back. But bragging to others is definitely out! It is others who must talk highly of your achievements and successes, not you yourself.

The fact of the matter is, most civilised and cultured people value modesty as a virtue. Not the kind of false humility we spoke of earlier, but genuine modesty, in the sense of underplaying one's successes. And the truth of the matter is, really successful people allow their successes to speak for them; and they are all the more impressive, because they do not show off in public. This is why we have the elaborate protocol of introducing our

Distinguished Guests to an audience. It is a well- accepted, well established practice, that allows us to bring out the achievements of the honoured speaker or dignitary before an audience, and invite their praise, appreciation and recognition for the same. In this case, it is we who are proclaiming his achievements, and that is entirely acceptable!

Why Do People Boast?

Why do people boast? If we do a thing well, where is the need to boast about it? It was indeed a wise man who gave us the proverb, "Empty vessels make the most noise". If only we realise how annoying and boring incessant chatter about oneself can be, we would all become followers of that wise maxim: "The best conversationalist is one who talks to you about – yourself!"

We are known by our actions, our attitude, the way we treat others, the kindness and courtesy we show to others. Our behavior and attitude are the best introductions we can give to ourselves. Why then do we need to boast about ourselves, our status and our accomplishments?

Alas, it sounds so simple and straightforward. But it is so difficult to put into practice!

"Do not turn your face from others with pride, nor walk arrogantly on earth. Verily the Almighty does not like those who are arrogant and boastful," the Holy Quran tells us. If you really wish to make friends and influence people, boasting cannot be the chosen way for you.

Alas, we live in a world where people feel that their power, their status, their position and their achievements need to be proclaimed from rooftops. Otherwise, they think, nobody will respect them.

I cannot help thinking that such an attitude springs from a very low sense of self-worth.

Thus says the Lord, according to the *Book of Prophets:* "Let not the wise man boast in his wisdom, let not the mighty man boast in his might, let not the rich man boast in his riches." And reinforces the same through the *Book of Proverbs:* "Let another praise you, and not your own mouth; a stranger, and not your own lips."

As I said, it is easier said than done!

Boasting for some of us, starts from childhood. "My Dad has a bigger car," or "My Mom is prettier than yours," are common childish boasts we hear in the playground. At the other end of the spectrum, we all have come across grandparents happily bragging about their grandchildren's achievements. Baby pictures and cellphone photographs are happily thrust before visitors' eyes and we do not grudge the proud grandparents our indulgence.

It is not just what is said, but the way in which it is said that causes problems. And there is a very thin line that divides healthy, happy pride from boastful arrogance. Monopolising a conversation to focus on our bragging is just not acceptable!

Recently, a friend brought me an article about "smoasters" – i.e. social media boasters! The writer pointed out that popular social media sites make even normal people boast, brag and show off with their 'status updates'. And it seems so easy, because they are not really boasting to anyone's face; it is all so anonymous to click a picture of yourself in front of the Vatican or the Statue of Liberty or the Eiffel Tower and to say, "Enjoying myself in Paris" or wherever. The British have a typical tag that invites envy. "How I wish you were here!"

A recent survey carried out in Britain confirms this. Many people admitted to clicking themselves at a famous landmark, uploading smug shots of themselves at the beach or enjoying a fancy meal at an expensive restaurant, all to show off to their friends. Many of them also added that they would only 'tag' themselves in a glamorous location which would make them look good.

According to the same research, quite a few people admitted that they would deliberately write a boastful holiday status to make people at home envious. Most of them defended their boasting, insisting that if they are happy they have a right to shout about it online. More than half said that it was fine to do it, because 'everyone else does it', and also admitted that they did it just because they think it's amusing to 'wind other people up'.

Why do people boast? I would say, it's human nature, which for some of us, can turn ugly, if not kept under checks and control. This is not asking you to suppress your instinctive expression, but to learn to respect others and curb excessive self-promotion.

Some people think that it is basic insecurity, a low self-esteem that makes people 'blow their own trumpets' as we put it rather uncharitably. To compensate for their insecurity, they speak and act in an arrogant manner.

I must also add that some people set excessive store by what others think of them. They need validation. Boasting is their way of ensuring that their worth and value are well known in their social circle. Little do they realise that it might have the opposite effect, by making people dismiss them as boastful braggarts.

We all need to share the good things we have done, we need recognition, love and appreciation from the people who matter to us. There are outlets available to us for this purpose; your parents, your spouse, your children, and your good friends, who know you and love you. It is always acceptable to share our triumphs and successes with them and celebrate the same with them. But let us curb our enthusiasm when it comes to boasting in public, or before all and sundry.

Some schools in the US send out what is known as a "Parents' Brag Sheet" to all their students' parents. The parents are invited to share with the school Counsellor all the things that they consider special about their child, his/her accomplishments, best qualities and habits and any personality traits which they consider to be exceptional. They are also invited to share anecdotes and experiences to prove the points they are making. Here are some of the questions from a Brag sheet:

1. What has your child accomplished during the past three or four years that is most meaningful to you? (Please do not recount your child's resume.) Please share any anecdotes and specific examples you think would be helpful.

2. What do you consider to be the personality and character traits that make your child special (i.e. communication skills, willingness to take risks, social skills, leadership style)? Whenever possible, please add anecdotes.

3. In what area do you feel your child has shown the most development and growth?

4. If you had to describe your son/daughter in five adjectives, what would they be and why?

PRACTICAL
SUGGESTION
NO.2

REFRAIN FROM TOO MUCH TALK.
PRACTISE SILENT SELF-AFFIRMATION

May my ego be silent. So I can hear what others say.

- Robin Sharma

Silence is Golden

Four monks decided to meditate silently without speaking for two weeks. By nightfall on the first day, the candle began to flicker and then went out. The first monk said, "Oh, no! The candle is out." The second monk said, "Aren't we not supposed to talk?" The third monk said, "Why must you two break the silence?" The fourth monk laughed and said, "Ha! I'm the only one who didn't speak."

Each monk broke the silence for a different reason, each of which is a common stumbling block to meditation. The first monk became distracted by one element of the world (the candle) and so lost sight of the rest. The second monk was more worried about rules than the meditation itself. The third monk let his anger at the first two rule him. And the final monk was lost in his ego.

You could have ended the story at the point when "the candle flickered and went out."

The four monks have each broken their silence for an altogether different reason. But another side is in the fact that the fourth monk spoke at all. Had he simply maintained his silence, he would've been successful in his endeavor. But if he had, in all likelihood, the other three would've probably continued to argue and not even noticed his silence. I know many people who are like this monk; their motto: If I'm doing something good and no one is watching (or no one notices), I might as well not be doing it at all. They believe that the reward is not in the effort, but in the recognition.

Were I a fifth monk I would wait 10 minutes into the exercise, stand up and yell loudly. HAAAAAAH I LOSE!!!! Then walk out to do some non-competitive meditation.

John Suler

Silence is Precious

The Practice of Silence is one of my favourite ideals and I have written and spoken about the same whenever I could. But silence in relation to the conquest of the ego has a different focus altogether. Ego pushes people to talk too much, to talk constantly about themselves and to dominate conversations by pushing their views and opinions on others. Asking such people to observe silence is almost akin to strangulating them! They would feel deprived, they would demand the right to be heard and insist that their voices and opinions are worth being heard.

Some of them may be right, some of the time. Rightly or wrongly, excessive egoism is associated with excessive talking – the sort of talking that does not allow others to get a word in edgewise, the sort of talking that drowns out other voices, the sort of talking that dismisses others' views with a contemptuous "Nonsense!" or "What rubbish!" or, even without any of these insulting comments, just raising the voice and talking incessantly.

Before we get into the merits and demerits of loud talking (I have a few friends who claim that they do not deliberately talk loudly; it is just that their voices are a little on the high-decibel side) I want to remind my readers of one indisputable fact: the more you talk, the less you listen; and the less you listen, the less you will learn.

Let me suggest a simple exercise. Look at yourself in the mirror, and talk loudly to yourself, as you would, if you were arguing heatedly, pushing your point of view in a meeting or uttering one of those insulting terms such as Nonsense or Rubbish. Speak those words to yourself in the same decibel level and the same force that you use to others. How do you feel? What does the spectacle of the image in the mirror shouting at you make you feel?

It is not just the loud voice that drowns you out; it is the accompanying egoism that is the force behind the raised voice that shocks and hurts people. And it is not necessary for you to raise your voice to get your point across or to assert your authority! When you let yourself go, when you let yourself be yourself in this shouting exercise before the mirror, only then will you realise how you sound to others.

I am told that cricket and tennis coaches make their athletes watch recorded videos of the games they have played (both matches which they have won and lost) to understand their strengths and weaknesses in the sport and the forced or unforced errors they have committed. This visual replay enables them to understand their weaknesses much better than a whole sermon on where they went wrong or what their wrong moves were.

Listening to yourself can also be a salutary exercise. You can also ask your trusted friends whether you tend to be a little loud.

A sister once said to me, that when she got the first phone call from her daughter who had gone abroad after marriage, she was so excited that she raised her voice unconsciously. Her son's school friend who was visiting them, said to her, "Aunty, your voice does not have to reach the UK. It only has to reach the mouthpiece of your telephone."

The lady admitted that she was a little ashamed but also self-conscious to realise that she had raised her voice to that extent. And, let us not forget, she was not reproving or reprimanding anyone, or arguing with anyone. She was just excited!

An excited voice might hurt our ear drums; but an angry or bullying or authoritarian voice might cause much more damage. And I stress this point again: a loud voice is not the only way to assert one's authority.

Many people equate loudness with power and authority. They believe mistakenly that a soft voice or a mild demeanour can be construed as weakness. A leader, they point out, has to be assertive and forceful.

Leadership does not have to be 'louder'ship!

A loud voice may instill fear; it may embarrass, humiliate or belittle the person you are talking to: but does it produce the desired result that you wish to achieve?

My advice to you would be to try a firm, no-nonsense, but toned down approach. This way, your message is delivered clearly and it goes home effectively. This is where silent self-assertion comes in.

Imagine that you are faced with an employee/subordinate/assistant who has repeatedly erred, made mistakes, refused to take your instructions properly. You may well argue, "I would be less than human if I did not lose my temper with one such person!"

That is as may be. But what is the purpose of your yelling? To get the work done; to get the desired results. So when he comes before you having made the same mistake for the nth time, try a little silent self-assertion. While you count ten mentally to curb your rising temper, tell yourself, "I shall get through to him; I will make him understand the problem; I will try a little patience, I shall try a little firmness, I shall make my instructions explicit; I will get this work done out of him."

Experts point out that being assertive is neither being aggressive, nor being menacing; if you are loud and aggressive, you will be regarded as a bully; people will imagine that you are yelling because you are frustrated. But if you are firm and assertive, people will know that you respect them but that you mean business and they will respond to your orders in the right way.

There is a lovely story that a friend narrated to me. A holy man was visiting the city of Varanasi and went to take a dip in the sacred River Ganga. As he reached the bathing ghat, he found a family group on the bank of the river, shouting in anger at each other. He turned to his disciples and asked, "Why are these people so angry? Why do people shout so loudly?"

His disciples thought for a while, and one of them said, "Maharaj, I think people lose their temper and yell because they have lost their calm."

"But I don't understand," insisted the Guru. "Why does anyone have to shout when they are standing right next to the person they are talking to? Now, if one member of the family stood here on the bank and another was in a boat in the middle of the river, I can see that there is a need to shout, in order to attract his attention. But when the other person is just next to you, why do you have to lose your voice? You can save your throat and talk to him softly, can't you?"

The disciples offered many answers but none of them were satisfied by any of the explanations.

Finally the saint explained, "When two people are angry with each other, their hearts distance themselves from one another. There is a gap, a chasm. One has to shout to be heard across that chasm. The more angry they are, the greater the emotional distance between them, and they can only communicate by shouting."

The saint smiled. "Have you seen two lovers talking to each other? They only whisper, or they simply communicate with their eyes. That is because their hearts are very close. The distance between them is either nonexistent or very small..."

He looked at his disciples and said, "Even friends and family members have differing points of view. Why, even married partners may have a bitter quarrel. But when you argue, you must not let your hearts get distant. You must not utter words that would increase the distance between you. If you do not follow this simple rule, there will come a day when the distance is so great that you would have lost the close relationship and you will not find the path to return. This is how separation and divorce come about in marriages."

You Are Not Always Right

Dr. Wayne Dyer observes: "When you let go of the need to be right, you're able to strengthen your connection to the power of intention. But keep in mind that ego is a determined combatant. I've seen people end otherwise beautiful relationships by sticking to their need to be right. I urge you to let go of this ego-driven need to be right by stopping yourself in the middle of an argument and asking yourself, 'Do I want to be right or be happy?' When you choose the happy, loving, spiritual mood, your connection to intention is strengthened. These moments ultimately expand your new connection to the power of intention. The universal Source will begin to collaborate with you in creating the life you were intended to live."

Some people feel that they have the right answer, the solution to the problem being discussed. How then can we refrain from putting our point of view across, they ask. How can we just keep silent when our raised voice may actually lead to a diffusion of the crisis?

To these friends I say again: do not underestimate the power of silent assertion. Visualise tempers cooling; visualise the crisis dissolving;

wish with all your heart and mind for harmony and peace to be restored among the people you love. Put your point of view across patiently and firmly. You will find that this gets you greater acceptance than raising your decibel levels!

Above all, realise that you don't have to win by shouting others down. This is a clear case of win-lose situation. Try instead for a win-win situation. Be gracious and allow the other person to feel that he is part of the solution.

The ego always seeks to dominate or control others, even in very subtle ways. Therefore it is also super sensitive to being dominated. Whenever we give an idea or suggestion to others, the tendency is to raise immediate resistance. Instead, try to silently affirm what you want to suggest or propose. A silent affirmation in the mind, with or without actual mental words, is far more powerful than the spoken word. It directly reaches other people. Often they will express the very idea you are affirming as their own suggestion and be far more enthusiastic because they perceive it as their own.

- The Mother's Service Society

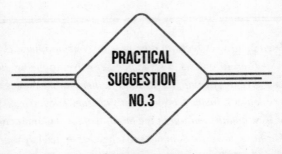

PRACTICAL SUGGESTION NO.3

OFFER AND ACCEPT CRITICISM IN THE RIGHT SPIRIT

Criticism may not be agreeable, but it is necessary. It fulfils the same function as pain in the human body; it calls attention to the development of an unhealthy state of things. If it is heeded in time, danger may be averted; if it is suppressed, a fatal distemper may develop.

- Winston S. Churchill

Never Take Offence

Uday Singh had a Bachelor's degree in commerce, but could not find a job. Desperate to earn a livelihood, he decided to start something of his own. He managed to borrow a meagre sum of money, and after a great deal of effort, he set up a small shop with sundry garments.

On the first day, he sat in agonizing wait for the first ever customer. A wealthy and fashionably dressed woman walked in, browsed through his stock and complained, "This place has nothing but bits and pieces," and walked out. Uday did not take offence or get angry; in fact, he thanked her and the next day, put up a board outside the shop saying, 'Bits and Pieces'.

His business began to flourish by selling miscellaneous items.

Taking Constructive Criticism

Each one of us is sensitive; each one of us is different; and each one of us is constantly variable - our mood and temperament change from day to day, may be even from hour to hour! And yet we have evolved into a society, into a community, into a global habitat with families, institutions and corporations.

This has been possible with time, a growing sense of awareness, and a great deal of understanding, tolerance, sympathy and mutual respect.

Our social and intellectual evolution did not happen in a flash; nor was it a smooth, slow and steady process. We had flashes of brilliant achievement; we had distressing failures and drawbacks; our great inventors and path breaking thinkers faced a lot of disapproval and criticism. We grew and evolved as a species because our great achievers took criticism in the right spirit!

Constructive criticism actually helps us to improve ourselves and become higher achievers and better human beings. If we accept criticism in the right spirit and look at things with a new and positive perspective, we will benefit immensely.

More often than not, we put a negative connotation on the term 'criticism' in daily life. We equate the word with pointing a finger, finding fault, or commenting on the shortcomings of someone's efforts.

Can we avoid criticism? Yes. According to Aristotle, we can avoid criticism by saying nothing, doing nothing and being nothing!

How many of us would like to take on a life of nothingness?

In personal life as in professional life, we often face criticism. We can use it constructively, to improve ourselves and overcome our weaknesses; or we can take it negatively, and become victims of stress, frustration and low self-esteem.

The Book of Proverbs in the holy Bible tells us: "A man who refuses to admit his mistakes can never be successful."

On the whole, it is unrealistic to imagine that we are perfect and that we cannot do or say anything wrong! To err, as the saying goes, is after all human. We all make mistakes; sometimes, costly mistakes. But the wonderful thing about life is that it gives us an opportunity to learn from our mistakes and become better people. This is why it is good to listen carefully to all criticism levelled against you and understand how it can help you improve.

Criticism arises out of people's perception of something you have said or done. You may have meant it all for the best, but at that point in time, others perceived you differently. Criticism will help you step back and look at yourself from another's perspective. Then criticism becomes a learning experience for you!

The way in which you handle criticism is an important indicator of your maturity and poise as a human being.

How to Handle Criticism

1. Do not take everything personally. Look at the situation and the issues. We all love to be praised, and when there is something to celebrate in the family or at work, we are happy to receive praise and compliments. If the teacher criticises your handwriting, you cannot equate yourself with your homework. If you criticise your wife's cooking, she must not identify herself with a badly made dish or dessert.

2. Do not react in stress or anger. Maintain your balance and calmness and listen to the other person with patience and respect. Even if the criticism levelled against you is unfair or malicious, there is no need to hit back! The situation will then spiral out of control and may even turn ugly. Should you feel that you are beginning to lose your temper, turn away and leave the room with a polite excuse. This will diffuse the tension and allow you time to gather your thoughts.

3. Don't pay attention to the tone or the attitude of the critic; pay attention to what he says. Most criticism tends to have an element of truth in it. Ignore the aggression and the confrontation of the other person and examine his suggestions carefully. Detach your feelings and detach the other person's anger, if he shows any.

4. Value criticism as much as you respond gratefully to praise. Norman Vincent Peele once said, "The trouble with most of us is that we would rather be ruined by praise than saved by criticism." Flattery and hypocrisy, insincere praise and exaggerated compliments are no good to us. If we wish to evolve, to grow and develop as better human beings, we should learn to value criticism and appreciate the people who tell the truth as it is.

5. There are times when unfair, untrue, malicious criticism is levelled at us. It is important that we remain detached from such people and such comments and ignore them with dignity. It is useless wasting energy on such false accusations. The cardinal rule here is to be polite and cool while you refute the unfair criticism.

6. Respond; do not react in haste. It is better to allow a little time to elapse before you respond to a critic who has been unfair. Let the bitter feelings of anger and injured ego subside before you offer a correction or justification.

Learn to Appreciate Rather than Criticise

Just because you happen to have been the recipient (or victim!) of excessive criticism, don't become a harsh and unforgiving critic! Fault-finding, constant criticism and magnifying the mistakes of others are poor, ineffective ways of changing the world. When we focus on others' faults, we only draw those negative forces unto ourselves.

When we constantly criticise others and find fault with them, we hurt them with tongue-lashes, which, in some cases, are worse than whip-lashes! An ancient poet tells us that the tongue is a very powerful instrument. It should be used largely for uttering the name of Lord. Instead, if we use the tongue only to find fault with others, we are abusing the God-given power of speech and language. The poet adds that there are four grievous wrongs that our tongues can commit:

(1) Uttering falsehood (2) Scandal mongering/ gossiping (3) Finding fault with others, and (4) Excessive talk.

When I find fault with others, I regard myself as superior – better than the others. This is pride, this is egoism. This must be overcome if we are to be truly happy.

If you wish to be happy, you can begin by thinking, "Everybody has something good in him; there is something that I can learn from every human being."

We have ingrained notions of what is right and wrong, what is proper and improper, what is acceptable and unacceptable. When we impose our narrow and harsh judgments on others, we condemn ourselves to a critical attitude and lose out on a lot of good cheer and joy that comes from being open-minded.

As I said to you earlier, none of us is perfect. No man or woman can ever be perfect. Even Jesus said to us, "Call me not perfect. Alone the Father in heaven is perfect!" Marriage, friendship, any relationship or business partnership involves two imperfect human beings trying to live together, work together or establish a link. Unless we learn to accept people as they are, we will lose all possibility of finding happiness in our relationships.

A stranger arrived at the gates of a city, which he was visiting for the first time. An old woman sitting on the roadside greeted him, "Welcome to our city".

"What kind of people live here?" the stranger asked her.

"What kind of people live in your home town?" the old woman asked him with a smile.

"Oh, they were terrible," swore the stranger. "They were mean, nasty, malicious and selfish. They were impossible to live with."

"You will find people here are pretty much the same," the old woman said to him.

A little later, another stranger arrived at the city gates, and was welcomed by the old woman.

"What kind of people live in this city?" the second traveller asked.

"How did you find them in your home town?" the woman asked him.

"They were a wonderful lot – hard working, friendly, and easy to get along with."

"You will find the people here likewise," the old woman assured him.

Approach people with love and understanding – and you will find the same reflected in their approach to you.

See the good in others! Utter kind words and loving thoughts about them. You will find that this has a healing effect on them and you! Harsh words and criticism causes people to shrink and wither. The happy, positive individual does not criticise, he does not find fault with others. If we too begin to see the good in others we will keep on growing better and better and our minds will always be at peace, and the world around us will smile.

And finally, a word for those leaders and superiors who don't have to listen to criticism from others. There are some businessmen and executives who feel that employees are spoilt by praise and that only constant criticism can keep people on their toes. If you are a leader or an employer, don't let ego dominate you! Don't undermine others just so that you may feel better or superior to the rest. You will only drive others away from you. You can lead from the front, setting an example for others to follow; you must not destroy another's self-esteem to establish your own! In an organization, team spirit, mutual respect and understanding can achieve a lot more than obsessive control and constant criticism.

I've always envied people who can graciously accept constructive criticism. It seems I was not born with that trait, and throughout my career I've struggled with receiving feedback, even when it was entirely accurate. At the moment I hear the words of critique, my heartbeat quickens and my mind begins to race — first in search of an explanation for this assault on my person and then for a retort to rationalize whatever actions are in question.

And I'm not alone. Unfortunately, in the heat of the moment, many of us react with defensiveness and anger or — even worse — attack the person giving us feedback. But the truth is, we need to get over it. We know there's value in constructive criticism — how else would we identify weaknesses and areas of improvement?—and being able to handle it calmly and professionally will only help us maintain relationships and be more successful in everything we do.

- Nichole Lindasy, Career Development Consultant

PRACTICAL
SUGGESTION
NO.4

LEARN TO RESPECT AND APPRECIATE OTHERS

There is no respect for others without humility in oneself.

- Henry Frederic Amiel

Dignity and Respect: A Child's Story

There was a buzz of curiosity and expectation at school. Everyone was talking about Amanda. What would happen to her? Would she be taken away from her parents and placed under foster care?

Amanda was just eight years old. She was always thoughtful and quiet. Her reading and math were good, and she would answer all the questions the teacher asked her in class. She was always neat and clean, but the clothes she wore were old, frayed and shabby. The school authorities had become concerned for her when they realised that she and her two younger brothers were living in a shelter for homeless people with their parents.

The children stared curiously as Amanda was called out of class to talk to the social worker from the county office. The social workers wanted to ensure that she was well cared for;that she might, if necessary, be placed with foster parents in a home setting, so that her education and personal growth would not be affected.

"When did your family shift to the shelter?" asked the social worker kindly.

"Oh, my father lost his job when the automobile factory closed down. And then, my mother lost her job as a daycare worker at the factory crèche. We could not pay rent and we moved to the shelter."

"But my parents are trying everyday to get themselves new jobs," she added quietly. "Even today, they have gone out to the agency on a call."

"How long can your family stay in the homeless shelter?"

The child grew thoughtful. "I don't know," she said softly. "But I'm sure it won't be for long…"

"So you don't have a home now?"

"Oh," brightened the little girl, "We have a home, we are together, only we just don't have a house to put it in."

The social workers left the school. Amanda was not taken out of her family or her "home".

With an innate sense of dignity, this little girl prevented a chain of events that may have been quite devastating to her and her family. I believe she taught the adults around her about respecting the power of family and love.

The social workers also learnt to respect the feelings of an underprivileged family. In the process, they ignored the letter of the law to give Amanda's family a chance.

Courtesy : dearfriendsblog

Appreciate others

Respect and appreciation for others is the perfect antidote to ego as well as negative emotions like depression, frustration, resentment and bitterness. When we fail to respect and appreciate our family and our friends, our spiritual evolution is thwarted, and our minds are darkened. Giving respect to others earns respect for us; appreciation and gratitude illumine us from inside, and brighten the environment we live in.

Appreciation also helps us grow in the spirit of tolerance and acceptance. The world we live in is far from perfect; we are not ourselves paragons of perfection; and the same goes for the people around us. As they say, it's a crazy, mixed-up world – but we must recognise ourselves as part of all this imperfection, and accept life as it comes.

I am afraid we are living a life of such egotistical and selfish preoccupation that we simply fail to appreciate others.

The neighbour who greets you with a bright smile and cheerful hello...

The domestic help or office attendant who is always pleasant and well mannered...

The Security at the gates of your society who unfailingly allows your vehicle to drive through with a friendly greeting and salute...

A warm, delicious and wholesome meal that your mother has cooked and kept ready for you...

A friend who asks you with genuine care and concern, "How are you?"...

Every day we are witness to acts of courtesy and kindness offered to us. Let us not dismiss them as small or trivial. They deserve to be appreciated!

It was George Mathew Adams who said: "He who appreciates another enriches himself far more than the one whom he praises. To praise is an investment in one's own happiness. The poorest human being has something to give that the richest could not buy."

When I find fault with others, I regard myself as superior – better than the others. This is pride, this is egoism. This must be overcome if we are to be truly happy.

It is our besetting fault that we often take others for granted. We eat what is placed on the table but fail to appreciate the person who cooked the meal. We lean on our friends for support, cry on their shoulders but fail to appreciate them for always being there for us.

Of a great English poet, I read that he never spoke a word of appreciation to his wife. So long as she lived he criticised her and found fault with everything that she did. Suddenly, the wife died. The poet was grief-stricken. He was ashamed that he had failed to write poems in appreciation of her, when she had been alive. "If only I had known," he lamented. "If only I had known..."

Truly it has been said, life is too short to be small. Let us not be small-minded. Let us be generous with praise, appreciation and encouragement.

Silent appreciation is not of much use to anyone. Therefore learn to express your appreciation. It is not enough to think that someone is being kind and good; a kind word unsaid is a kind thought wasted. Go up to people; reach out to praise them, thank them, appreciate them for what they have done and you will really make a difference!

A distinguished Professor of the Kellogg's Business School, Deepak Jain, observes: "A leader will be truly successful only when his subordinates believe that they can grow under him."

How best can this impression be conveyed to them? Surely by the leader's words of appreciation and encouragement!

Find Time For Others

There was a multimillionaire who prided himself on never wasting time with unnecessary things. He never offered a tip for any services; nor did he even bother to appreciate anyone for the help rendered to him.

His complicated finances had all been handled by his Chief Accountant, a man who had served him and his father faithfully for decades. One day, the accountant committed suicide. The millionaire was devastated. Where would he ever find anyone who was so committed, so sincere, so trustworthy?

The cash transactions and account books were found to be in perfect order, for the dead man was a meticulous worker. He had also left a brief note for his employer, which read: "In 30 years of working for you, I have never heard one word of encouragement from you. You must be very proud of that!"

If only parents, leaders, managers, bosses and husbands administered much needed doses of appreciation and encouragement, we would no longer have people who suffer from misery and loneliness and the feeling of being useless or unwanted.

All of us need to bask in the warmth of appreciation every now and then. Otherwise, our self-respect becomes endangered.

A young man who was about to begin his career was told by his father, "You must learn to give your best with or without appreciation. Don't let the quality of your work suffer because others do not praise you."

Sound words indeed. It is good not to expect appreciation for all that we do. But surely, nothing stops us from expressing our appreciation for others! Now for example, if the young man's bosses had been told "Don't be content with just paying your workers salary. Encourage them with your words of appreciation whenever possible!" What a world of difference it would have made to the young man's work!

Perhaps husbands are more insensitive, more lacking in this aspect that their wives. A survey of women in rural America revealed that farmer's wives had one common complaint; they were taken for granted. They were hardly ever thanked for what they did.

One of them narrated an amusing incident. Every day she took the trouble to make a delicious meal to set before her husband and sons, when they returned home from the evening. She learnt new recipes. She prepared complicated dishes. It was obvious that they enjoyed the meal for it disappeared in no time at all. But not a word of thanks, not a single compliment was forthcoming.

In exasperation, she made a meal of cattle feed and set it, steaming hot, on the table one evening.

"What's this?" they screamed, when they had downed the first mouthful, "Are you crazy or what?"

"I have waited 26 years and not heard a word of praise from you," she replied. "I never ever thought that you would notice the difference."

The Sufi Saint Jami tells us: "We can spend a whole lifetime enjoying various benefits and not appreciate their value until we are deprived of them."

Now give me one good reason why we should allow that to happen? Why should we allow ourselves to go through a loss just to realise the value of what we already have?

At work, praising others, passing positive news and appreciation about a colleague and sharing the news with others can benefit people all round: the person to whom you have conveyed the positive news, the person you have appreciated and last but not the least, you yourself! People will value the other person for the qualities you have highlighted: but they will also value you as a person who notices others, who is ready to give credit where it is due and who notices what is happening around him.

Look for opportunities to notice the good things that people are doing!

When you look for positive traits in others, you unconsciously attract those positive traits to yourself; conversely, when you are always trying to spot others' mistakes and their wrongdoing, you attract those negative traits to yourself. Therefore, I always tell my friends not to judge others harshly or criticise them constantly.

If you are genuinely someone who looks for good in others and appreciates them, your company will be pleasant to others; you will become a sought after colleague and friend.

When you tell your colleague, subordinate, child, husband or friend that they are wrong, that they are insensitive or that they have done something badly, you take away their incentive for improvement. On the other hand, when you are liberal with your encouragement and appreciation, they will do their best and surprise you with what they can achieve!

Making others feel good about themselves builds better relationships. This is what Lord Chesterfield urges his son to do: Make every person like himself a little better, and he or she will began liking you very much. Sincere praise reassures people. It dissolves the negative notions they have about themselves and improves their self-esteem.

Let's stop focusing on all that is wrong and focus instead on all that's right; let's stop cribbing about what we don't have and look instead at what's there for us; let's take the time to appreciate people for what they are and what they can do, instead of focusing on their defects. When we complain and criticise constantly, we are drawing negativities into our lives. Each time we utter something negative about people, work or life, we actually begin to believe it more and more, and make it come true in our lives. Our imagined ills become our reality. Needless to say, the reverse is also true. When we believe that life is good, people are good and things are going good, they become better, actually. When we visualise good, focus on the positives and talk about all that is positive, success actually begins to take shape for us.

Six Tips to Show Appreciation

1. *Be genuine about your praise and don't expect anything in return for being nice.*

2. *Be very specific with your words and use the person's name whenever possible. This makes it more meaningful. For example, "Bill, thanks for making us feel so welcome when we arrived at the hotel. It was the perfect start to our vacation."*

3. *Demonstrating eye contact and positive body language goes hand in hand with the words you choose.*

4. *Think of special ways to show your gratitude. For example, buy flowers or do something special for your spouse that you know he or she would love. You don't have to spend a lot of money for the thank you to have value.*

5. *Send a hand written thank you card or note of appreciation. Most people don't take the time to do this simple act.*

6. *If the praise or appreciation relates to a specific act or circumstance, give it as soon after the event as possible to have the most impact.*

- Todd Smith

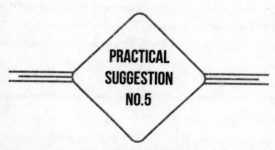

PRACTICAL
SUGGESTION
NO.5

REMEMBER — YOUR REAL VALUE LIES NOT IN YOUR OUTER, EMPIRICAL SELF, BUT IN YOUR INNER, IMPERISHABLE SELF

You cannot be lonely if you like the person you're alone with.

- Wayne W. Dyer

Do You Know Your Worth?

"Know your worth".

The phrase is so overused that it has almost lost its meaning. My fear is that many people – especially women – are saying this without truly being able to clearly define what their worth is.

If you told me, "I know my worth" and I asked you, "Well…what is it?" Could you respond with confidence exactly what you mean when you say "I know my worth"?

Try it. Try explaining your worth right now.

Knowing your worth is a continuous process and life-long journey. Why? Because, each and everyday we are bombarded with images and messages that will constantly make you question and doubt your worth.

You may say that just because you can't explain it, doesn't mean you don't know your worth. I strongly beg to differ. If you asked me how I paid for a dress I just bought, I can tell you with confidence that I paid $42 for it. That is the clearly defined value of the dress. That is how much it is worth. I can tell you the amount is determined by the brand, the store, where it was made, the material it is made with and the season we are in.

If we can't truly define our worth, then we really don't know our true value. I want to encourage women (and men) of God to stop just following fads and saying things because they sound good. Seek to know your true value for yourself. Don't just say you know it. You should be able to articulate it.

Have you ever been to a jeweler? Pick out a diamond, and they can tell you exactly what it is worth because of the cut, the shape, the amount of carats etc… They don't just say, "Well of course it's valuable, it's a diamond!" They have a clear reason why the diamond is priced the amount that it is.

How do I define my worth? That's the million dollar question. But even after you have defined it, it is more important to believe it and live it out. Sometimes we puff our head up with so much knowledge, but it doesn't ever make it to our hearts. But life experience will demonstrate and show you your value.

The list goes on and on, but knowing your worth and living it out all come from developing an intimate relationship with God and being intentional about blocking out anything that negates your true worth.

- Brittany Dixon

Cultivate Your Mind!

William Lyon Phelps was a distinguished writer and critic, as well as a popular Professor at Yale University. He had inspired and guided hundreds of students during his long and distinguished career.

When he was asked to write a message of guidance and inspiration for the American people, he asserted: "The principle of happiness is like the principle of virtue: it should not be dependent on things, but be a part of your personality."

When Professor Phelps had been a young student, he had drawn inspiration from the words of President Timothy Dwight who had visited his college and addressed the students. Dwight had told them emphatically: "The happiest person is the person who thinks the most interesting thoughts."

This was what he taught his students too. Real happiness cannot come from external things, he told them. The only lasting happiness that you will experience is that which springs from your inner thoughts and emotions. Therefore, he urged them, cultivate your mind. For an empty mind seeks mere pleasure as a substitute for happiness. It is essential, he said, to "live inside a mind with attractive and interesting pictures on the walls."

The happiest people are not the ones who make money, buy property and own stocks. The happiest people are those who cultivate their minds and think interesting thoughts.

Many of us are apt to equate happiness and success with money, material wealth and possessions. This is sheer ignorance. You cannot be happy just because you live in a mansion or a penthouse apartment. You cannot achieve peace and inner harmony just because you drive a BMW or Benz. You cannot be considered 'successful' just because you are a millionaire.

Supposing you were told, 'Today is the last day of your life. Make a list of all the things that you feel you have accomplished, all the things that have made you feel truly happy': what are the things you would put down in that list, knowing that you have only a few hours left to live?

I'm certain that your car, bungalow and bank account will find no place on the list! What you are sure to put on it would be the most fundamental elements of a truly happy life – your love for God, the love and

respect you have earned from your near and dear ones, the sunshine you brought into people's lives by your warmth, affection and compassion, the kindness you have received from your friends and the love and kindness you have shown to other people.

Happiness is an Inner Quality!

It was Abraham Lincoln who said, "Most folks are about as happy as they make up their minds to be." And since happiness gives meaning and purpose to life, we must know where to find it. All the world's greatest philosophers agree on this point: true happiness stems from within us, from a way of thinking about life. This is the most enduring, most agreed upon truth about happiness: if the principles of contentment and satisfaction are not within us, no material success, no pleasure or possession can make us truly happy, or give us a sense of high self-esteem.

A farmhouse in the countryside, a summer villa in the hills, your own yacht at the Boat Club, life membership of an exclusive club in the city – these are not the things that account for your self-worth! Living in a penthouse does not make you a better person. Driving a Porsche does not add to your happiness. Diamonds, gold, rubies, stocks, shares and mutual funds do not always guarantee peace and harmony in your life.

Alas, many of us regard these outer 'symbols' as indicators of our self-worth, our happiness and success. These material resources are not as valuable as your inner, personal resources.

The Walden Experiment

The great writer, Henry David Thoreau realised this two centuries ago, when he gave up his comfortable townhouse and went to live in the lap of nature, in Walden woods. The *mantra* of his life was: Simplify! Simplify! Simplify! Thoreau was a practising minimalist, before the term minimalism was even thought of!

As a young writer, Henry David Thoreau had felt stifled and miserable in the city of Concord, where he lived. He was a Harvard graduate, and he had started off as a teacher. But he wanted to lead a peaceful life, to devote his life to study, to thinking and writing. He found the society around him uncongenial for such an aspiration. Everywhere around him men were only in pursuit of one thing – material gains. People were interested only in piling up property and possessions, enslaving themselves to 'things' and 'goods' that really meant nothing to him.

Thoreau realised that the world's greatest thinkers and philosophers of the past had lived lives of Spartan simplicity. He decided to take a leaf from their books – he decided to leave Concord and live alone in the woods, cut off from all the artificial trappings of so-called civilisation; he would concentrate on improving his soul's estate.

In March, 1845, Thoreau set out for Walden Woods with a borrowed axe. He started building a cabin for himself on the edge of Walden Pond on a tract of land belonging to Ralph Waldo Emerson, his mentor. On July 4, the cabin was completed, and a vegetable garden planted. Carrying with him his flute, a few note books and pens and a copy of Homer, Thoreau moved into the cabin in the woods, to launch his experiment in simple living and high thinking.

"He chose to be rich by making his wants few," remarked his friend Emerson.

Let me tell you, this was not the life of retirement that a senior citizen seeks. Thoreau was just twenty-eight years old when he began his remarkable experiment. He was not a misanthropist, nor a hermit. He had many friends in Concord, but he wished to escape from the artifices of contemporary civilisation and live a free and independent life.

"The mass of men lead lives of quiet desperation," he wrote. "… Most of the luxuries, and many of the so-called comforts of life, are not only not indispensable, but positive hindrances to the elevation of mankind…"

He lived in Walden woods for a little more than two years. Having completed his experiment successfully, he returned to conventional, social life.

From his notes made in the woods, he produced *Walden,* the masterpiece which made him famous, and inspired Mahatma Gandhi.

I went to the woods because I wished to live deliberately, to front only the essential facts of life, and see if I could not learn what it had to teach, and not, when I came to die, to discover that I had not lived…

The record of an experiment in serene, simple living, Walden, is as relevant now, as it was 250 years ago. "Simplify your life," Thoreau urged his readers again and again. "Don't burden yourself with possessions. Keep your needs and wants simple, and enjoy what you have. Simplify! Don't fritter away your life on non-essentials. Don't enslave yourself for luxuries you can do without…"

What Do You Want From Your Life?

Sometimes, we allow ourselves to be trapped by our routine, outer life. We allow ourselves to fall into a rut of our own making, and think that we cannot get out. We are trapped in the vicious cycle of acquisition, buying bigger homes, getting bigger cars, taking more bank loans and credit card loans, calculating our lives and earnings in down payments and installments. If the neighbour takes a holiday abroad, we feel small until we have equaled his 'record'. 'This is my life,' we think; or, 'This is my job… I have to think of my promotion, I have to climb to the top, there is no escape from this for me… I am stuck with it . . . I have no options.' We become tired, depressed and cease to pay attention to our own feelings and inner aspirations. We are not listening to our hearts…

Occasionally at least, we must stop to ask ourselves: is this what I want out of my life? Am I equating my life with my possessions and my acquisitions? Are these acquisitions adding to my sense of self-worth? Are they making me really happy?

Some years ago, there was a talk in corporate circles of something called a downshift. That is, a slowing down of the pace of life, an alternative lifestyle sought by busy young executives who suddenly realised that they did not want to spend the rest of their lives just making money. Thus, strange 'downshifts' came to pass...

A thirty-year old couple who were high powered financial executives discovered the joys of cooking together. They gave up their lucrative jobs in a London bank and opened a cozy cafeteria in a seaside town. They laughed, played and worked together; they cooked and served tasty meals; they chatted with their customers and charmed everyone with their 'personal touch'. They never ever looked back on their lucrative careers.

A wealthy man from France took a vacation in a Himalayan resort. The peace, tranquility and the clean mountain air so appealed to him that he decided to live and work there as a ski instructor.

A research scientist from an American University happened to hear an Indian spiritual teacher talking about meditation and silent prayer.

The scientist felt his inner being transformed. He accepted the teacher as his Guru and became a devoted volunteer in his *ashram*.

These people listened to their inner voices. They were not carried away by the dazzle of money and by their jet setting executive lifestyles. They thought about what they wanted out of life. They asked themselves what they would like to do, what they would love to do – and they followed the dictates of their hearts. Money, power, position were all secondary.

I can hear some of you saying, "It's alright for millionaires and eccentrics from western countries to 'downshift' and get away with it! What about Mr. and Mrs. Average citizen? What about the Common Man with his multiple responsibilities and commitments?

I am not suggesting friends, that all of you should give up your jobs and open sandwich bars down town! All I'm saying is that these people discovered that making money was not enough to bring them happiness, and so sought alternate lifestyles and occupations which may not have been as rewarding financially – but offered greater satisfaction and contentment.

Many of us are trapped by the blaring noise, the glaring lights and the mechanical routine of a demanding society. We are surrounded by the buzzing of alarms, the ringing of telephones, the clatter of the keyboard, the loud volume of the TV, the high decibel levels from the speakers, horns, engines, cars, buses and trucks. The glare of the TV screen and artificial lighting are constantly hurting our eyes. We get up like mechanised robots and go about our daily routine listlessly.

You don't have to quit your job to make a change! Think of the activities you enjoy. Do you like writing? Then begin to write short stories, poems and articles. Do you enjoy singing? Join a music group and take lessons in classical instrumental/vocal/western music. Do you enjoy theatre? Join a drama group. If you love animals, volunteer to serve with Blue Cross, SPCA or a local animal shelter. Do you love reading? Offer to read for the visually disabled or to the inmates of a Home for the Aged. Do you love babies? Volunteer to help out at a Balgram-SOS children's village. Do you love going to the temple? Offer to assist the devotees who throng the local temple during the peak hours. Do what you love – find joy in activities that appeal to your heart, and not merely to your head . . .

Exercise your soul! Turn to nature to nurture you. Learn to spend at least a little time every day in outdoor activities – it can be something as simple as walking, or just sitting in a garden bench. Being in touch with the healing forces of nature helps to restore calm, peace and a sense of harmony to your life...

The demands and distractions of modern life only take us away from ourselves. This is why Indian philosophy and culture insist on silence, withdrawal, stillness and meditation whereby you can discover the Divine within yourself.

The great Norwegian dramatist Henrik Ibsen said: "Money can buy the husk of things, but not the kernel. It brings you food, but not appetite, medicine but not health, acquaintances but not friends, servants but not faithfulness, days of pleasure – but not peace or happiness."

Man does not live by bread alone!" Ruskin wrote. Making money, accumulating possessions can never lead to a fulfilling life. Of course it is good to have some of the luxuries that money can buy – but we would be the losers if we miss out on all the wonderful things that money cannot buy!

"The more a man finds his sources of pleasure in himself, the happier he will be," writes the philosopher Schopenhauer. "...The highest, the most varied and lasting pleasures are those of the mind..."

Truly, if we cannot find our sense of self-worth, our true happiness and contentment within, it is useless to seek it elsewhere!

Seek ye first the Kingdom of Heaven
and all these things shall be added unto you.

- Jesus Christ

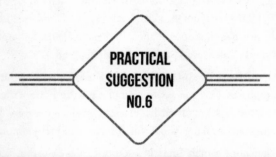

PRACTICAL SUGGESTION NO.6

CULTIVATE FRIENDSHIP WITH THIS INNER SELF. IDENTIFY, UNDERSTAND AND TRANSCEND THE EGO!

When we transcend the ego, we realise that we have a higher self beyond our limited view of our individual identity. It means that we no longer see our identity as simply an individual consciousness, but rather that we are the consciousness that moves through all things.

When we transcend the ego, it doesn't mean we kill the ego. Transcending the ego does not mean waging a war against the ego. It means that we move to a higher context of self and include our individual self as well. Egolessness does not mean the absence of a functional self, it means one is no longer exclusively identified with that self.

- Jonathan Mead

Wisdom and Humility

The great Indian saint and philosopher, Adi Shankaracharya, was walking up the Himalayas along with his disciples. On the way, they passed by the vast river Alaknanda in spate. As they stopped to marvel at the swirling waters and the mighty flow of the river, one of the disciples remarked: "Gurudev! This sacred river and its magnificent flow is as nothing compared to your vast knowledge, which is as vast as the mighty ocean!"

Shankaracharya smiled at this exaggerated compliment. Still smiling, he dipped the edge of the staff he was carrying into the eddying flood, and then held the stick out to show to his disciples. A few drops of water dripped from the stick.

"Look at these few water drops that are dripping from my staff," he said to the disciples. "That is all the knowledge that I have gained from the vast ocean of knowledge."

The disciples were stunned into silence. "What can I say to you about my knowledge?" said the saint. "You saw that barely a few drops of water clung to my staff when I dipped it in the river. So it is with all of us. All that we know, and all that we have learnt is just like this small drop when compared to the vast ocean of knowledge present in the universe."

The Truth About the Ego

Beware of those who feed your ego! They may please you with their flattery and honeyed words. But you have to be on your guard to take these words with that proverbial pinch of salt.

If the ego is within us, the means are also within us to transcend the ego!

I have always maintained that there are two selves within each one of us: the lower self of the passions, pride, ego and negativities; and the higher self of noble aspirations, love, truth, harmony and beauty. It is up to us to discard or discipline the one and cultivate the other!

The name 'Rabia' means beautiful. Beautiful was the life of Rabia, although she was born to poverty and darkness; beautiful was her soul, for she walked the sufi way of devotion, love, detachment, humility, patience, gratitude and surrender.

Sold into slavery as a very young child, Rabia faced hardship and privation which would have hardened the heart of any other girl: but this saintly soul bore her misfortunes with courage and fortitude. Her selfless spirit and her indomitable faith secured her freedom from slavery. Her deep devotion and intense faith worked miracles for her in her daily life, and she was worshipped as a saint, even in her lifetime. Yet she chose to live a life of poverty and simplicity, refusing all offers of financial support.

One day Rabia was sitting on the banks of a river, meditating on the Divine. *Dervish* Hassan happened to pass by. Seeing Rabia praying on the banks of the river he said to her, "Rabia, why are you praying on the banks of the river? Let's offer worship to the Lord on the waters of the river." The truth of the matter was that Hassan had acquired extraordinary powers, whereby he could stay afloat on the water. He wanted to demonstrate his power to Rabia and the world.

Confident of the spiritual power that could help him achieve miraculous feats, *Dervish* Hassan forthwith threw his prayer mat on the river. The prayer mat made of straw floated on the waters! "Come Rabia", he called to her, "let's get on the prayer mat and offer our prayer to the Lord."

Rabia was quite unmoved by the feat. She felt that it would only be a public display to impress people and not really an exercise in meditation. She said to Hassan, "If you want to meditate on God, I have a better way." Rabia then threw her prayer mat in the air and said to Hassan " Come, let us rise in the air and meditate."

Hassan was mortified by Rabia's gesture. He had actually wanted to make her admire his feats and powers; but she had overwhelmed him with hers. He said to Rabia in all humility, "I cannot perform a miracle in air, for my *siddhi* (spiritual energy) is limited only to the water." To this Rabia replied, "What you can do even a fish can do; and what I can do, a tiny fly can also do. But we are neither fish to float in the water, nor flies to fly in the air. Let us not forget the real purpose and the true goal for which we have received this human birth. These are mere tricks and we must not waste our precious human birth in working them."

King Janaka and Sage Ashtavakra

There is a beautiful story that reinforces this idea in our ancient scriptures. King Janaka had a dream. He dreamt that he was a beggar, destitute and starving. He was in the throes of extreme hunger, indeed acute starvation. He woke up with a start and was profoundly moved by his dream. He asked himself: What is the Truth? Who am I, am I the king who dreamt that he was a beggar, or the beggar who is dreaming that he is a king?

Determined to get to the truth, he summoned all the sages and scholars as was his wont and requested them to give the answer to his question – offering half his kingdom for a satisfactory reply. Many scholars came, for many were tempted by the consideration of the hefty reward offered: no less than half the kingdom. But not a single one of them could provide a suitable answer to the king's question.

Sage Ashtavakra arrived at the King's assembly hall and announced that he could answer the King's query.

Raja Janaka said to the young sage in all humility, "Please enlighten me, wise one."

Ashtavakra said to the King. "They tell me that you are going to give away half your kingdom in return for an answer that you seek to your question. But you must tell me how you can do this – does this kingdom belong to you?"

Taken aback, the King replied, "But of course it belongs to me; I have inherited it by due rights by my royal lineage."

"May I ask who owned the kingdom before you came to the throne?"

"My father."

"And before that?"

"My father's father".

"And, after you?"

"My sons will inherit this kingdom, even as I did."

"So you see, mighty king, this kingdom did not belong to you earlier, and it will not be yours in the future. Yet you claim ownership in between, and even assume the right to give a part of it away…"

The king realised that there was a serious flaw in his assumptions, and that he was actually only the caretaker of the kingdom and that it did not belong to him. Ashtavakra had made it clear to him that he could not give away what he did not own.

"Now tell me, what will you give me if I answer your question?"

The King replied in a small voice, "I offer you my body, which is my own."

"Oh King, you are making the same mistake again," laughed Ashtavakra. "Are you sure you are the owner of this body?"

"Yes, of course, I am the dweller in this body, therefore I own it, and everything is under my control."

"May I ask you, where was this body of yours 100 years ago and where will it be 100 years from now?"

Again the king had to concede that the body did not really belong to him either and that it was just given to him on loan by Mother Nature for the duration of a lifetime, after which it would have to be returned to Nature.

"Alright, said the king, "I'll give you my mind."

"You think you own your mind; you cannot even control your mind. How can you give something over which you have no control? You tell your mind to do this and it does not even listen to you?"

Eventually King Janaka realised that he was in the presence of a great Master, and asked to be accepted as Ashtavakra's disciple to be taught the mysteries of the Self.

The essence of the dialogue between King Janaka and Ashtavakra is beautifully rendered in the *Ashtavakra Gita*.

Many of us are given to making tall claims: "I know this," "I can do this," "I am so and so, such and such is my designation," "I am such a one," "I am the doer," "I am the giver," – how vain and futile are such assertions!

Here is how a great poet saint puts it:
When my ego was struck by the sword that is the Guru's love,
That love began to kill my ego.
Even when I was alive, I experienced death.
My death died; and I became immortal.

The ego is subtle; its workings are not obvious. As the seeker is making progress on the path, he may pride himself on his efforts. Sometimes he thinks he is close to success. Sometimes he feels he has attained his goal. Sometimes he realizes with despair, that it is very difficult to be spiritual.

Then comes to him the realization that his efforts and endeavours are not pure but tainted, spotted. The darkest spot of them all, he realizes, is the ego – the lower self – the 'I'. And then he begins to realize that he must transcend the ego to enter into the Limitless. He begins to realize that of his own accord, he can do nothing, achieve nothing. He learns to accept all that comes to him – abasement, criticism, disappointments – as the Will of God. As the love of God and Guru fills him, egoism dies. When this happens, he is reborn – born again in the life of thespirit.

This, I humbly submit, is the essence of *dwija* – one who is twice born. He is born once in the flesh; he is reborn when he realises that he is not the body he wears!

This is what happened to King Janaka. He learnt this great truth from one sage; he passed it on to others!

King Janaka also serves to illustrate the point that higher awareness is not the exclusive prerogative of a certain 'type' of people – people who are unworldly, committed to self-enforced poverty, prone to asceticism, self-denial or given to renunciation. People in power, people wielding authority, wealthy and influential people can take to this higher awareness, this perception of the inner self, if they so desire. Equally, householders, businessmen, scholars, office workers and students too, can take to cultivating friendship with this inner self.

Each one of us has the indwelling *atman;* so each of us is free to make friends with this true self; our awareness is all that it takes to transcend the ego, the lower self and cultivate the spirit!

As long as we identify ourselves with the ego-self, the physical body and this material life, we cannot find true happiness. We must stop being obsessed with the physical, material, sensual aspects of life.

The more we identify with the body, the more unhappy we become!

Have you seen a stagnant pond that has no outlet and does not flow into a canal or stream? Its waters become stale, dirty and covered with thick moss; it begins to smell bad; it becomes the habitat of frogs. So it happens with a life that does not flow out through good deeds performed for others' benefit; it too become stale and stagnant with vanity, ego, selfishness and desire. But a life that is spent in the service of others, flows clean and free like a sparkling river and ultimately reaches the ocean of the Supreme Self. Thus, doing good to others, serving others, always turn out to be the best that one can do for oneself!

Cultivate the soul through service! In other words, become aware that you are only an instrument of God. He is the One Worker—you are but His tool, His agent. Therefore, renounce all idea of egoism, of the narrow self and become an instrument of the eternal *shakti* that shapes the lives of individuals and nations.

It is good that those who seek to serve others bear this in mind: that service is meant to purify the mind, heart and intellect, and to move us on the path of God-realisation. They are also blessed with the unique, selfless joy that comes from serving those in affliction, and bringing the light of love into dark, unhappy lives. These are the genuine feelings to be nourished by those who save others—and not vanity, ego and self-seeking pride.

Let me appeal to you: do not seek to serve others to prove your superiority. This brings disgrace to you and it degrades those whom you 'serve' in this spirit. It destroys the very spirit and concept of service. True service is free from the contamination of the ego.

It is my view, therefore, that detachment from the physical, and awakening to the inner self, is the first step to transcending the ego and finding the true happiness that is our birthright.

Consider the term *sat-chit-ananda* or true eternal bliss. Is permanent, lasting, real happiness possible for us if we dwell on the material plane? If we are worrying about our bank balance, thinking of our next pay cheque, envying our superiors at work and constantly comparing ourselves with others?

The gift of life has been bestowed on all of us, that we may find fulfillment and grow in perfection.

Life is wonderful! If you feel that your life is not wonderful, and needs to be changed for the better, you must cultivate friendship with the higher self, the true self within! Joy, love, purity, peace, prayer, contentment, acceptance and the selfless spirit of service must permeate your life; then you will find that your world will change, and your whole environment will shape itself in accordance with your persistent thinking.

Therefore, let us transcend the petty ego that makes us miserable and envious and insecure and make our lives truly wonderful. Let us –

1. Realise what we are in essence.
2. Count our blessings.
3. Become "thank you" people, cultivating the spirit of gratitude to God.
4. Appreciate others.
5. Stop pushing ourselves forward all the time.
6. Help as many as we can on the rough road of life.
7. Learn to put ourselves last – whenever we can!

Fighting with your ego by will just makes it stronger. By declaring war on it, you make an enemy. A simple example: You wake up in the morning, and it's raining and gray, and the mind says, "What a miserable day," and this is not a pleasant thought. You likely feel some emotion: dread, disappointment, unhappiness. You suddenly realise that your judgement of what kind of day it will be is based on a mental habit, an unconscious default. That simple awareness creates space for a new thought to emerge. You can look again out the window without that preconception and just see the sky. It's gray. There's some sunlight filtering through the sky. There are, perhaps, raindrops falling. It's not actually miserable at all. It has a certain beauty. Then suddenly, you're free. You're no longer imposing something on reality, and you're free to enjoy what, previously, you had rejected.

- Eckhart Tolle

AFTERWORD

The Virtue of Humility

Very often, I have heard these words again and again ringing in my heart:

Learn just one word,
Forget all else,
Let your heart be pure,
All else you have learnt
Matters little!

We spend so much time reading books of all kinds: books of our special interests, books to update our professional knowledge, books for entertainment, and so on. But books have their limitations. I say this advisedly, for I too am a book lover! Still, I do not hesitate to tell you, that book learning is at best limited learning. True, we acquire knowledge from books. But it is abstract knowledge arising from dry words. We acquire knowledge. But all knowledge is not wisdom. And, the reading of books does not always cleanse the heart and the mind. The volumes of words we read ultimately become a burden which we are unable to carry.

In one of our ancient scriptures, a comparison is drawn between a man who is a great scholar and a donkey bearing a load of sandalwood!

A scholar may have read hundreds of books, he may have gathered extensive knowledge, but if this knowledge cannot be transformed into wisdom and translated into deeds of daily living, then he is little better than a donkey carrying a bag of 'sandal wood' on his back, unaware of its fragrance and value.

There are scholars who are continuously engaged in the pursuit of knowledge. But, alas, their learning only makes them proud and egoistic! This is not true learning. *Vidyadadhativinayam:* True knowledge teaches us humility. This is the one word we must learn, the one virtue we all need to cultivate!

Once, we put a question to Gurudev Sadhu Vaswani: what is true knowledge, the absolute knowledge, the greatest wisdom? Gurudev Sadhu Vaswani replied, "True knowledge is the realisation that I am nothing, He is everything. This realisation makes man humble and gentle. And there is no wisdom greater than this."

Gnana (true wisdom) is not gathered from books, but from inner life. This, our ancient *rishis* cultivated, and the Guru is one who can impart to us – not merely the text, not merely the 'sayings' and words – but the distilled essence of that wisdom. But to be worthy of absorbing that wisdom, a true disciple, a true *sishya,* must be truly humble!

The great Chinese sage, Lao Tse, expresses this thought in beautiful words: "How does the sea become the king of all rivers and streams? Because it lies lower than they!"

When the Sikh Temple, which is now known the world over as the Golden Temple, was being built at Amritsar, Guru Arjan Dev's disciples said to him: "Master! Let this Temple be the loftiest in the land!"

The Guru replied quietly, "Let the Temple be lower than all other buildings. What is humble shall be exalted. The branches of a fruit-laden tree, bend low to the earth."

He who has conquered the ego, does not regard himself as superior to others. He believes in the divinity of each individual. He is at harmony with himself and others. The burden which most of us carry all our life, the burden of the self and desires, he has laid aside. He is ever calm and serene. Only he can regard himself as a seeker – a true disciple.

He has to learn many new things. But, what is most difficult of all, he has to unlearn many things he has learnt.

A scholar came to a saint and said, "O seer of the secret! Teach me to live the Life Divine!

The saint said to him, "Go and unlearn what thou has learnt and then return and sit before me!"

He who would be a seeker, he who would walk the path of discipleship must walk the way of humility. He must give up the opinions he has formed, the standards to which he is accustomed. The things the world worships – rich food, fine houses, costly clothes, the applause of men, honours and titles – are as nothing to him.

Of Rabbi Hurwitz it is said that when he was appointed as the Rabbi of Frankfurt, he was given an overwhelming reception. Thousands of people joined in the procession to do him honour. When a friend asked him how he felt in that hour of triumph, he replied, "I imagined I was a corpse, being borne to the cemetery in the company of multitudes attending the funeral!"

The truly humble man must die to the world, must die to the ego. His self must be annihilated, before he can be filled with the Guru's grace.

It is not just ordinary mortals like us, who are afflicted with the ego. Great people also have their ego. If you have a small ego, it is easy to vanquish, and your suffering will also be small. But if you have an enormous ego, it is going to cause you a great deal of pain and suffering before it is done away with!

It is the same with 'surgery'. The removal of a small growth like appendicitis or tonsillitis only involves a minor surgery. But if it is a major growth, it will require a major surgery!

Gurudev Sadhu Vaswani said to us, "An egoless man is one who walks the little way. His is the way of acceptance. He accepts everything. If he is asked to be the president of the country, he accepts it and holds the reins of the country. And when he asked to be sweeper, he accepts that too, in the same measure. A humble man asks no questions."

Gurudev taught us many lessons in a similar way. He would assign a certain job to each one of us, and then without giving a reason, he would hand the same assignment over to someone else. Those of us who were gentle and humble did not question him. But the others would argue and ask him for an explanation. Gurudev Sadhu Vaswani would face their queries and their arguments with a sweet smile. "Learn to accept!" he would tell us again and again. "A humble man will always have this prayer on his lips: O Lord! Give me the strength to accept Thy Will."

A devotee, who regularly attended the Mission congregation, once donated large sums of money towards the service activities of the Mission. He insisted that his name should not be announced, nor the amount mentioned in the Mission. One day, Gurudev said, "Make an announcement of the donation in the *satsang*." When the announcement was made the man became angry. Gurudev smiled at him and said, "True humility knows no pride. To be humble, walk the little way. To be humble, is to seek refuge in the Lord." A truly humble man thinks of himself as nothing. He believes that his Guru is everything and that his duty to serve his master and accept all his commandments.

Yogi Mahadev did not have any disciple. One day, a young man approached him and begged him to accept him as his disciple. To this the yogi said, "I will accept you as my disciple on one condition. Go to the peak of the mountain and jump from there." The young man was stunned. He said, "If I jump from the peak of the mountain I shall die." The yogi smiled at him and said, "Unless and until you die, how would you be re-born?" The young man pleaded, "Please explain." The yogi replied, "To understand this you will have to go to a farmer. He will explain it to you. It is only when the seeds are totally buried that the new crop comes up."

The young man nodded – and went away, never to return!

What are the marks of a true disciple, we asked Gurudev Sadhu Vaswani. The Master outlined the following traits:

- Humility: When a true disciple was asked whether he was such-and-such-a one's disciple, he answered, "I am trying to be his disciple, so help me God!"

Humility helps us to avoid several obstacles and evils on the path of discipleship – such as ostentation and pretension.

- Obedience to the teacher: The disciple must always remember that in obeying his Guru, he obeys God.

The teacher may put the pupil to severe tests. The worst may be this – that he asks the disciple to be far away from him. For a teacher knows that a raw fruit requires both sunshine and shadow, in order to ripen in maturity. So too, the disciple must have the double experience of fellowship and separation: for in separation too, there is union. Spiritual obedience to the teacher, not physical nearness to him, is the mark of a true disciple!

- *Seva* or service: the disciple must serve the teacher whole heartedly.

Growing in humility, obedience and service, the disciple will develop intuition and rise to meet his Guru on the spiritual plane.

Intuition is the power to see on the inner plane. When this power develops, the disciple does not argue: he easily understands his teacher. The disciple learns to 'feel' intuitively, the wishes of his teacher. The teacher may not utter a single word. So it was that the Master said: "My own hear My voice."

A true disciple becomes less and less argumentative: when his legitimate questions have been answered, his genuine doubts cleared, he becomes more and more intuitive. He loses himself in the Guru.

A man of God was once asked: "What is the way to God?"

He replied, "When thou hast vanished on the way, then thou hast come to God!"

So the disciple too, must 'vanish': vanish to the ego and vanish to the lower self of pride and passion, so that he may be prepared to see the Light!

If only we would look around us, we will see how Mother Nature presents to us the very picture of humility. How humbly and lovingly she serves every creature that breathes the breath of life! When we tread on the lawn, we crush the tender green blades of grass under our heavy footsteps. But the grass revives again to receive our steps. Water is the source of all life; without it we would all perish. So powerful is the flow of water that it can drown people, when a river is in spate. And yet, water always flows down from a height; it never ever flows up from below.

The laden tree, it is said, always bows low. True it is that the tree full of fruits is always the one to be stoned by people who wish to eat its fruits. And yet the tree gives us its juicy fruits in return for the stones we cast on it; and it gives us shade where we may sit and eat its fruits.

Therefore if we wish to acquire the virtue of humility, let us learn from Mother Nature. The light of God shines in all of us, in every creature that breathes the breath of life. But in some of us, the divine light is hidden behind many veils, so that we cannot behold its radiance. These are the veils of pride and ego. When these veils are torn asunder, we can see the divine light shining in all its glory. Humility will surely help us see this Light!